"Not far from the center of the American Continent, midway between the oceans east and west, midway between the Gulf and the Arctic sea, on the rim of a plain, snow swept in winter, flower decked in summer, but, whether in winter or in summer, beautiful in its sunlit glory, stands Winnipeg ... City of the Plains, from which the eyes of the world cannot be hid."

RALPH CONNOR, 1909

"The most important thing in life is not the triumph but the struggle. The essential thing is not to have conquered but to have fought well."

BARON PIERRE DE COUBERTIN

Pan Am Proud

A Tribute to Champions

The Official Commemorative Book of the 1999 Pan American Games

Published by

DT Publishing Group INC.

THE GLOBAL CONNECTION

Panasonic Canada Inc. is part of the world's largest electronic corporation. It is a member of the Matsushita group, which is owned by Matsushita Electric Industrial Co. Ltd. of Japan. When the company was founded more than 80 years ago by Konoske Matsushita, he believed that in order to become a successful businessman it was essential to develop products that consumers would want to make their lives easier and more enjoyable. Also by making these products in abundance he could keep the price down, thereby allowing more people to purchase them. As a result, Matsushita Electric was able to contribute to society in two ways by providing the products that improve and enrich people's lives and then using a percentage of the net profits to be channeled back into education, the arts and other just causes. This was the foundation of the Matsushita business philosophy.

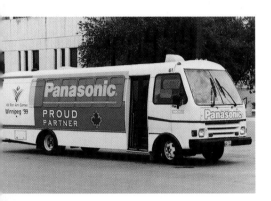

From three employees and a double-socket light bulb fixture in 1918 to more than 275,000 employees in 300 companies worldwide, the company has come a long way. Thousands of products with the brand names of Panasonic, National, Quasar, Technics or RAMSA have been developed by Matsushita Electric and millions of people around the world continue to enjoy them.

THE ROLE OF MATSUSHITA IN CANADA

For more than three decades, Panasonic Canada Inc. has built a strong reputation as a leader in providing state-of-the-art consumer electronics technology to the Canadian market, under the brand names of Panasonic and Technics. Additionally, the company markets business-to-business solutions including among others: notebook computers, office copiers and fax equipment, broadcast and professional audio and video systems and industrial components.

Aside from leading-edge technology, Panasonic has a proud history of corporate commitment in community affairs and culture. The company's program initiatives range from local arts, culture and education to sports sponsorships. In addition to being an Official Partner of the 1999 Pan American Games, Panasonic has been an Official Worldwide Olympic Sponsor since 1988. In 1995 and 1996, the company was the Official Partner to Canada's National Rowing Team and for two years leading up to the 1998 Winter Olympics, Panasonic was a sponsor of the Canadian National Snowboard Team. Since 1996, Panasonic has been a proud sponsor of the Stop Racism National Video Competition, a program endorsed by the Department of Canadian Heritage.

Panasonic Canada Inc. began sales operations in Toronto with seven employees in 1967 and has grown to more than 550 employees today. It is one of the best performing sales companies within the Matsushita Electric corporate family. Panasonic sales offices are located across Canada in Toronto, Montreal, Calgary and Vancouver.

Pan Am Proud
A TRIBUTE TO CHAMPIONS

MADE POSSIBLE WITH THE SUPPORT OF THE FOLLOWING PAN AM GAMES '99 SPONSORS

TITLE SPONSOR

Panasonic®

GOLD LEVEL

The Free Press

SILVER LEVEL

 Investors Group™

BRONZE LEVEL

XEROX SPORTEC
www.sportec.com

 Manitoba Hydro CentraGas Igniting the SPIRIT of the GAMES

Great-West Life

PATRON LEVEL
Henry Birks & Sons Inc.
IBM Canada
Industry Trade & Tourism (Explore Manitoba)

PAN AM PROUD - A TRIBUTE TO CHAMPIONS
WAS ALSO SUPPORTED BY THE FOLLOWING
FRIENDS OF THE '99 GAMES

GOLD LEVEL

 GEMINI
fashions of canada ltd.
 Winnipeg Commodity Exchange
 CARGILL

BRONZE LEVEL
CanWest Global Communications Corp.
KPMG LLP, Chartered Accountants
True Value Hardware and V&S Department Store
Wardrop Engineering Inc.

DT Publishing, Inc. acknowledges with thanks the host of additional writers and photographers who contributed to the production of this publication. Special thanks to the Winnipeg Free Press for its contributions.

Copyright © 1999

PAN AM PROUD - A Tribute to Champions
published by DT Publishing Group, Inc.

DT Publishing Group, Inc.
132 Main St. E., Suite 1
Grimsby, ON L3M 1P1
Tel: 905-309-1639
Fax: 905-309-1640

For book orders: **1-800-725-7136**

Printed and Bound in Canada

Canadian Cataloguing in Publication Data

Pan Am Proud - A Tribute to Champions
ISBN 0-9686013-0-8

PUBLISHER & EXECUTIVE EDITOR
Jeffrey A. Tiessen

ART DIRECTION AND DESIGN
Norman Lourenco

MANAGING EDITORS
Tiffany Morris
Kimberly Tiessen

ASSOCIATE EDITOR
Hilda Hoch

TEAM PHOTOGRAPHERS
Norman Lourenco, DT Publishing Group, Inc.
Daniel Galbraith, Concepts to Applause
Donovan Gaudette, Concepts to Applause

PRODUCTION ASSISTANTS
Laurene Hildebrandt
Brenda McCarthy

SPONSORSHIP SALES AND MARKETING
Jeffrey S. Yamaguchi
Promedia Communications Inc.

PAN AM PROUD - A TRIBUTE TO CHAMPIONS

CONTENTS

JEFFREY A. TIESSEN

PUBLISHER

This is a book about people. Proud people. Spirited people. It is about heroes - celebrated and unsung. It is about athleticism. It is about volunteerism. It is a tribute to the Americas' champions who competed on Winnipeg's Pan American stage. It is a tribute to a city that spent ten years building that stage and to the coral-shirted champions who flawlessly serviced it for seventeen days.

To be a Canadian in Winnipeg during the 1999 Pan American Games meant that your heart thumped a little faster, you stood a little straighter and you shed your traditional reluctance at patriotism and waved our flag wildly. To be a Winnipegger meant even more.

There were blissful moments for all Canadians to relish, perhaps the most enduring being cyclist Tanya Dubnicoff, the hometown girl whose obvious enthusiasm and pride in being part of the event ascribed "Games ambassador" status upon her. There was Manitoba's first gold medal of the Games, Emma Robinson's brilliant rowing achievement, and a victory over a momentous health concern. There was Graham Hood, the Canadian flag draped over his shoulders, applauding the packed stands at the University of Manitoba stadium after his gold medal performance. There was the uninitiated women's gymnastics team that inspired themselves to victory. And the Games' wunderkinds, the spirited and galvanized Canadian baseball team, playing with an exuberance that was as contagious as it was intoxicating.

There were doleful moments too... the heartbreaking one-run defeat at the hands of Cuba's hardballers ending our boys of summer's dream for gold and an Olympic berth. There was the emotional farewell from retiring Winnipeg racquetballer Sherman Greenfeld, a 10-time national champion. There was the heart-wrenching aftermath at the women's Team Handball gold-medal match that saw Canada lose its emotional quest for Olympic qualification. And of course, hockey's rollercoaster ride through the thrill of victory to the agony of tainted defeat.

There were innumerable and uncounted random acts of kindness. One could not have participated in the Games without being directly affected by the commitment and hospitality of Winnipeg's citizens - smiling, enthusiastic, helpful official volunteers or otherwise. These were the "People's Games." The Pan Am bar has been raised.

Congratulations Winnipeg. Be proud all of you.

H. SANFORD (SANDY) RILEY, CHAIRMAN
DON MACKENZIE, PRESIDENT AND CHIEF EXECUTIVE OFFICER

For 17 thrilling days in the summer of 1999, the Americas joined together in Winnipeg for the XIII Pan American Games, an outstanding celebration of sport and culture. From July 23 to August 8, Manitoba's capital hosted more than 5,000 athletes and thousands of coaches, officials, media, special guests, and visitors from 42 countries in the spirit of competition and friendship.

Community spirit was at the foundation of the Games' success; by rekindling the spirit of the 1967 Pan Am Games, the people of Winnipeg and Manitoba rose to the challenge and accomplished something that was shared with Canadians coast to coast and with people around the world.

The governments of Canada, Manitoba and the City of Winnipeg, together with a generous corporate family and supportive business community, demonstrated tremendous commitment to the Games. They, combined with the Games' 20,000 dedicated and enthusiastic volunteers, showed what Winnipeg was capable of when the community worked together toward a common goal. The results of their efforts are reflected in these pages.

Winnipeg shone on the world stage in 1999, and the stars of the Games are many: the athletes, who, in the name of sporting excellence, competed to the best of their ability; the coaches and officials, who lent their expertise in the name of sportsmanship; and the local, national, and international performers whose talents transcended borders and brought people together. This book pays tribute to them all.

The Pan Am flame has once again been extinguished, but the spirit of the Games lives on. Each of us will relive our special Games moments as we turn the pages of *A Tribute to Champions*.

MESSAGE FROM GARY FILMON
THE PREMIER OF MANITOBA

The XIII Pan American Games have now become a part of sports history, but the friendships and memories will endure long into the future. These games symbolized what we can and will do as we work together to make the next century our century in Manitoba and Canada.

Over 20,000 volunteers and supporters made it possible for Manitoba to host the largest sports and cultural event in Canadian history! Canada had its best medal showing of all time!

Above all, every one of the athletes from across the Americas reminded us that the journey to Winnipeg was not measured in miles, but in determination, perseverance and courage. Their strength of character symbolized the potential that can exist in all of us if we never lose sight of a dream.

MESSAGE FROM GLEN MURRAY
THE MAYOR OF WINNIPEG

On behalf of my colleagues on City Council, I salute the thousands of volunteers who contributed so much to the success of the Pan American Games. The tremendous support from Winnipeg citizens who turned their summer holidays into an opportunity to meet and assist visitors from all over the world is truly inspiring. The highlights of these Games are many. We celebrate the outstanding performances of athletes reaching for, and achieving their best, both as individuals and teams. We salute the coaches and families of these athletes who spend so many years actively nurturing the talent of their young people. Thank you for the memories, and again, congratulations to everyone who helped make the Pan American Games such a success.

INVESTORS GROUP INC.

Proud Sponsor of the 1999 Pan American Games

A TRIBUTE TO CHAMPIONS

Investors Group is proud to be an Official Sponsor of the XIII Pan American Games in Winnipeg. Our theme, *Remember how great it will be*, sought to rekindle the spirit of international sportsmanship and friendship Winnipeg experienced when it hosted the V Pan American Games in 1967.

Although much has changed over the past 32 years, one very important thing did not: that was the commitment and inspiration of the thousands of volunteers who gave so willingly of their time and their hospitality to welcome the athletes, coaches, officials and guests of 42 Pan American countries.

We are also proud that Investors Group employees and Representatives played an important role in these Games, as organizers, volunteers, spectators, and even medal-winning athletes. Special congratulations to Investors Group Representatives Colin Abbott of St. John's, Newfoundland who won a gold medal as part of Canada's national softball team, and to Wayne Sorenson of Calgary, Alberta who won the silver and bronze medals in the Free Rifle Prone and Air Rifle Men's events respectively.

Through these pages we celebrate the championship spirit of athletes like these, along with the invaluable contribution of the volunteers and the supporters in the stands who together made these Games so memorable.

WINNIPEG FREE PRESS

The Pan Am Games in Winnipeg in 1999 took $100 million of government money and 20,000 volunteers. It was, as those numbers suggest, a mammoth undertaking. No event of its size had ever been held in the province. It dwarfed Winnipeg's earlier hosting of the games, 32 years before. It was the spirit of 1967, however, that the games organizers intended to recreate.

In the weeks and months leading up to the games, it seemed doubtful that the city would come alive in the way it had in 1967. Ticket sales seemed slow. The quality of athletic competition was in doubt. Nervousness grew, and then suddenly evaporated.

From the opening to the closing ceremonies, the spectacle of the games took over. The athletic competition was fierce and full of surprises. Sometimes the favourites won, sometimes there were upsets, occasionally there were disappointments, but the spirit of the athletes, the volunteers and the entertainers who performed at Winnipeg's favourite spot where its major rivers meet, was second to none.

Winnipeg's slogan is "one great city". We proved beyond doubt that as a tournament centre, we are not just one "great" city, we are the "greatest".

NICHOLAS HIRST
EDITOR, WINNIPEG FREE PRESS

PAN AMERICAN GAMES HISTORY

When 5,000 of the Western Hemisphere's best athletes arrived in Winnipeg in July 1999, they were set to compete in the 13th version of the Pan American Games - Games that are second in size only to the Summer Olympics. When the Games began on July 23, 1999, Winnipeg became only the second city to host this event twice. The city first held the Pan Ams in Canada's centennial year, 1967; Mexico City hosted them in 1955 and 1975.

The first Pan American Games were held in 1951, but their history dates back two decades earlier. In 1932, the South American delegation of the International Olympic Committee (IOC) proposed the formation of an organization to promote amateur sport in the Americas. The idea led to the first Pan American Sports Congress in Buenos Aires, Argentina, in 1940. The sixteen countries represented at the meeting formed the Pan American Sports Committee. The first Pan American Games were to take place in 1942 in Buenos Aires, but World War II forced their postponement. The idea was kept alive, and at the 1948 Olympics in London, a second congress was held, renewing the commitment to hold Games for the Americas. The first Pan American Games opened on February 25, 1951, in Buenos Aires, featuring 2,513 athletes from twenty-two countries.

The organization governing the Games was renamed the Pan American Sports Organization (PASO) in 1955. It is currently comprised of 42 nations from North, Central and South America and the Caribbean. PASO is headquartered in Mexico City.

VOLUNTEERS

SINCE 1951, THE PAN AMERICAN GAMES have been anything but predictable. Champions have fallen and new talent has been launched onto the world stage. Each venue has had a distinct flavour and a new set of stars.

'51 BUENOS AIRES   Pan Am I   19 sports   21 nations   2,513 athletes

The Pan American Games concept was premised on better preparing Western Hemisphere athletes for the Olympics. The Second World War dashed the planned 1942 debut and after two more false starts, Argentina dominated the inaugural event.

'55 MEXICO CITY   Pan Am II   17 sports   22 nations   2,583 athletes

Canada's first participation in the Pan Am Games netted 11 medals: four gold, four silver and three bronze. Canada placed fifth overall behind the United States, Argentina, Mexico and Panama. Beth Whittal was a double gold medallist for Canada in swimming, winning the 400-metre freestyle and 100-metre butterfly.

'59 CHICAGO   Pan Am III   18 sports   24 nations   2,263 athletes

The United States was ridiculously dominant, with 237 medals, 128 of them gold. Canada was third best in total medals with 46, one behind Argentina. Coming off U.S. Open and Wimbledon victories in 1958, American tennis star Althea Gibson, won gold in Chicago.

'63 SAO PAULO   Pan Am IV   19 sports   22 nations   1,665 athletes

Canada was second overall in the medal standings with 68 - 11 gold, 28 silver and 29 bronze - to the United States' 219. The U.S. captured every swimming gold medal.

'67 WINNIPEG   Pan Am V   19 sports   29 nations   2,361 athletes

Canadian swimming's "Mighty Mouse", Elaine Tanner, earned two backstroke gold medals and set a world record. She shared the limelight with a new American torpedo, Mark Spitz, who won five golds. He went on to astound the world with seven gold medals at the 1972 Munich Olympics.

'71 CALI   Pan Am VI   17 sports   32 nations   2,935 athletes

The Columbian government spent an unprecedented $100 million (U.S.) to modernize the city founded by conquistadors in 1536. Canadians won 20 swimming medals, seven of them gold, and Canadian equestrians took six medals in six events, four of them gold.

'75 MEXICO CITY   Pan Am VII   19 sports   33 nations   3,146 athletes

This was the big test for Sport Canada's crash course in developing athletes for the Montreal Olympics. Canada sent the largest team ever to leave its shores - 349 athletes. It paid off with 91 medals, 19 of them gold. Californian Bruce Jenner, won gold in the decathlon. He set a world record the next year in Montreal.

'79 SAN JUAN   Pan Am VIII   22 sports   34 nations   3,700 athletes

Temperamental U.S. basketball coach Bobby Knight was arrested after getting into a fight with the local police. Edmonton swimmer Graham Smith won six golds at the 1978 Commonwealth Games, but could only manage silver and bronze in San Juan and lost his 200 individual medley world record to an American.

'83 CARACAS   Pan Am IX   25 sports   36 nations   3,426 athletes

The introduction of antidoping technology caught 19 athletes and sent scores more scurrying home with mysterious injuries before they were to compete. A clean Ben Johnson could only manage a sixth in the 100-metre.

'87 INDIANAPOLIS   Pan Am X   27 sports   38 nations   4,453 athletes

U.S. President George Bush opened the Games, but Cuban boxers closed them amid a near-riot. Anti-Castro expatriates taunted the boxers in the stands and defaced a Cuban flag. Canada won 161 medals, 30 of them gold.

'91 HAVANA   Pan Am XI   27 sports   39 nations   4,519 athletes

For the first time, Cuba toppled the United States in the gold-medal race, 140 to 130. U.S. athletes, uncomfortable with staying on Fidel Castro's island, opted to shuttle in from Miami. Cuban officials had to acquire sports equipment from Canada because U.S. suppliers couldn't deal with them.

'95 MAR DEL PLATA   Pan Am XII   34 sports   42 nations   5,144 athletes

At the Argentina Games, Canada had its best medal total in Pan Am history, 162. Argentina spent over $100 million (U.S.) putting on these Games, but when protective padding was needed for the railings at the speed skating oval, workers arrived with 11 bed mattresses.

'99 WINNIPEG   Pan Am XIII   41 sports   42 nations   8,949 athletes

Two-time Pan American champion cyclist Tanya Dubnicoff led 624 Canadian competitors into the Games. It was the third largest athletic competition in North American history, behind the Los Angeles Olympics in 1984 and Atlanta Olympics in 1996.

F or seventeen fantastic days, Winnipeg was the centre of the Western Hemisphere. Nothing the city could not handle. Winnipeg, affectionately referred to as the "Heart of the Continent", is well accustomed to playing centre stage. Geographically situated at Canada's centre, Winnipeg rests halfway between the Atlantic and Pacific Oceans. With Manitoba as Canada's most culturally and ethnically diverse province, home to the largest French-speaking population in Canada outside of Quebec, and the largest First Nation population in Canada, its capital city was decorously prepared for the largest celebration of sport and culture ever known in Canada. The city had hosted before. Its notoriously friendly folk would be the cogs in the wheels of the 1999 Pan American Games. Even the weather would be requisitioned. The sunshine capital of Canada did not disappoint. With incomparable pride and spirit, the City at the Forks played the consummate host to the Americas.

SETTING THE STAGE

SPIRIT OF '67

The first Pan American Games were held in Buenos Aires in 1951. The Games were intended to provide new opportunities for linkages among the nations of the Americas, as well as to offer amateur athletes a competitive venue between the Olympiads. Argentina had attempted to initiate the Games in 1940, and had succeeded in organizing an event scheduled for 1942, when the Second World War intervened.

Various obstacles after the war held up inauguration for some years, but once begun, the Games grew consistently. In 1951, 19 sports involved athletes from 21 countries. By the third Games held in Chicago in 1959, 24 countries sent 2,161 athletes,

including 298 women. In 1967, 29 countries were represented in Winnipeg.

In 1958, Winnipeg mayor Stephen Juba appointed an exploratory committee to consider whether Winnipeg could possibly host the Pan American Games. In 1959 Winnipeg put forth a bid for the 1963 Pan Am Games, but finished a strong second behind Brazil in the voting. The local group was then encouraged to turn their attention ahead to 1967. They did, much to the credit of James Daly, manage to hold the same committee together for the next four years. Their patience was rewarded as Winnipeg won the vote to stage the '67 Games.

Soon after, a management committee, consisting of local community leaders, was appointed to organize the event. It was headed by W. Culver Riley as volunteer president of the Pan American Games (1967) Society and by Daly as executive director. Behind this group were dozens of committees and thousands of volunteers, as Winnipeg sought to take advantage of its reputation as the Canadian capital of volunteer activity.

Organizing and administrating the Games was no easy task. Along with their colleagues, Daly and Riley tapped into their military backgrounds for guidance. They planned and executed the Games like a group of generals mapping out a major offensive. It was an approach that Daly felt was unique and effective. The 1967 Pan American Games were organized on a grass-roots basis with major sectors staffed almost entirely by volunteers. The same spirit which had beaten the rising waters of the Red River in 1950 was harnessed for less defensive purposes.

An army of over 9,000 people were responsible for everything from officiating to selling programs. Only 20 of those cashed a cheque as part of the Games' payroll. Volunteers had not only done most of the organizing work for the Games, but were also active in a variety of ways seen and unseen during the period of athletic competition. More than

200 doctors and dentists were on call, and 66 registered nurses did 494 hours of duty. Hundreds of Boy Scouts drawn from all over North America and housed in Birds Hill Park, put in more than 25,000 hours of service as "go-fors." One hundred and sixty volunteer interpreters made themselves available on a 24-hour basis. Ham radio operators kept some of the athletes, especially the Venezuelans whose country experienced an earthquake mid-Games, in touch with their families. A cabaret at Fort Osborne was staffed by Winnipeg musicians who played for three weeks of go-go dancing. Dozens of Winnipeg girls volunteered as dancing partners for the athletes, who were chiefly male.

According to Daly, bringing the Games to Winnipeg was a tremendous endeavor, mostly because the city wasn't equipped with a lot of the necessary sporting infrastructure. What facilities it did have had to be upgraded; what it didn't, needed to be constructed. "I saw the Games as a chance to get sporting facilities that we were lacking at that point built," said Daly, a longtime track-and-field participant, coach and manager. "We were going to be left with a legacy of facilities the community desperately needed."

Winnipeg would require a 50-metre pool, cycling oval, international-class track and field surface and a venue big enough to host the opening and closing ceremonies. The results were as such: the Pan Am Pool, the Velodrome, the unprecedented Tartan Turf track surface material at the University of Manitoba, coupled with a state-of-the-art tim-

ing facility, and the curved grandstand at the north end zone of Winnipeg Stadium which infused seating capacity at the facility. Many other local facilities - such as tennis courts and stands at the Winnipeg Canoe Club - were upgraded to international standards. "We must have done the job right because the swimming pool still has a reputation of being a fast pool," boasted Daly, adding that the U of M track and Velodrome all produced records during the Games and for years after at provincial and high school meets.

Tartan Turf was not the only innovation at Winnipeg's '67 Games. Another important breakthrough was in the extensive use of women as umpires and officials. Winnipeg's Marilyn Redekop became the first female official at an international-level men's volleyball match when she umpired the game between Canada and Mexico.

Ironically, the local bid was not without its critics, most of which were Winnipeg residents themselves. Daly recalled that his highest hurdle leading up to the Games was trying to change the mental psyche of the community: "When we suggested something like the Games, a lot of people were fearful that we couldn't afford it or couldn't do it properly, and would end up embarrassing ourselves."

To overcome this barrier, Daly spoke publicly an average of 150 times a year for five years to promote the Games. He remembers interest and, more importantly, confidence growing as the event neared. He maintains that personal stubbornness helped him overcome a lot of negativity he faced from the public. "The biggest satisfaction was seeing the attitudinal change in the city," he recalled. "My greatest pleasure was seeing so many other people pleasantly surprised about their own community, and their own country."

The relatively short lead time before the event, the lack of experience of the organizers, and the heavy use of volunteers all combined to cause some difficulties. Some advance organization was perhaps less evident than it ought to have been, and among the problems caused by lack of experience were the relative absence of international television coverage and difficulties of postal communications. The organizers did not put the world broadcasting rights out to bid early enough, and by the time they did so, the American networks were not interested. CBC televised the Games, largely for the Canadian audience.

But the 1967 Pan American Games in Winnipeg may be best remembered by some for something no one could have predicted or prevented. On July 23, 1967, organizers awoke to discover dark clouds and a constant heavy rain, the day of the Opening Ceremony. The traditional torch was on its way.

The torch had been brought by Canadian Pacific Airlines from Mexico City to Winnipeg, and then to St. Paul, Minnesota, which stood in for Sao Paulo. A team of 10 Canadian aboriginal runners carried the torch from St. Paul to Winnipeg, running 80 miles a day at an average speed of ten miles per hour. They arrived at Winnipeg Stadium exactly on time. As Prince Philip - who was to officially open the Games - stepped out of his automobile, the sun momentarily broke through the clouds. But he, Prime Minister Lester B. Pearson, and Manitoba officials got thoroughly drenched as they rode in an open convertible around the infield of the stadium. The rain continued throughout the afternoon. One sportswriter commented that Prince Philip well reflected the spirit of Winnipeg. "He stood there, soaking wet and pretended he didn't even know it was raining."

Given all the cliff-hanging that had preceded the Games, it is said that the actual athletic competition seemed at times, almost anticlimactic. There had been some concern over ticket sales, but in the end, a total of $862,172 in sales, representing over one million seats, was the best any Pan Am Games had ever done. Most of the ticket buyers were Winnipeggers themselves.

The Canadian athlete who won the hearts of the fans was swimmer Elaine Tanner, the "Mighty Mouse" from British Columbia. She won two gold medals and several others, setting records in the process. Other Canadian gold medallists included cyclist Marcel Ray in the 110-mile road race, and Harry Jerome in the 100-metre race. Jerome's was a photo-finish and a Pan Am Record. The United States beat Cuba for the baseball championship.

According to Daly, the 1967 Games gave the city the physical and mental wherewithal to move forward in many areas. In 1967, for example, Bishop Grandin Boulevard was home to gophers, rabbits and foxes; not cars and trucks. The downtown skyline didn't include such cement icons as the Trizec Building, TD Centre, or Fort Garry Plaza. There was no Convention Centre or Linden Woods, and Winnipeg Stadium had yet to be equipped with upper decks.

What directly spurred the growth and expansion in the city since then is debatable. However, Jim Daly knows a good starting line when tracking the last three decades of progress. It was the summer of 1967, a year he remembers fondly because he was finally able to watch an eight-year undertaking unfold. As host of the 1967 Pan Am Games, the risk and vision shared by people like Daly created a boon for the community for years to follow. What the city experienced for a period after the Games was proportionate to the impact Expo had on Vancouver and the 1988 Winter Olympics on Calgary. Long after athletes from the 29 countries had returned home, Winnipeg was left to enjoy several world-class facilities. The city also experienced a dramatic increase in tourism revenue, stimulated economic gain, and most importantly, renewed civic pride. "For a number of years afterward we were running around with our chests puffed out," reflected Daly. "I wasn't surprised the Games were a success."

Dan Galbraith

FROM CONCEPT TO COMPLETION

THE HISTORY OF WINNIPEG'S 1999 GAMES BID

Hosting the 1967 Pan American Games was a defining moment in Winnipeg's history. It is believed that hosting the 1999 Pan Ams will prove to be an equally important milestone for the city. Many of those credited with winning the bid to bring the America's Games to Winnipeg for the second time in just 32 years have very vivid memories of the first sports festival.

A 27-year-old Don MacKenzie stood in Winnipeg Stadium's parking lot in 1967, guiding cars into available spaces, thinking that being part of the Pan Am Games was like sharing in a small part of his city's history. Never could he have imagined that he would guide the 1999 Pan Am Games as Chief Executive Officer. Nor could he have imagined being escorted to a reserved seat for the Opening Ceremony alongside a princess - Princess Anne of the Royal Family - and a president, Mario Vazquez Rana of the Pan American Sports Organization (PASO).

Susan Thompson chauffeured the Mexican soccer team around during the 1967 Games. She had them to her home

VOLUNTEERS

for a barbeque. Elected as Mayor of Winnipeg in 1992, she vowed to do anything she could to bring the Games back. Thompson was the honourary chairwoman of the 1999 Pan Ams. And Sandy Riley: his uncle W. Culver Riley chaired the 1967 Games. Sandy was a teenager then, and a volunteer at the rowing events. Could he have imagined that he would someday captain the Pan Ams as chairman of its board of directors? He remembers what the 1967 Games did for his parents' generation; now he will discover what the 1999 Games will do for his contemporaries and the ranks of his children.

The 1967 Pan Am Games were not only a significant achievement for PASO, but for Winnipeg as well. The event left a legacy of facilities, pride and volunteerism which was sustained for three decades. It was only natural then, that when thoughts returned to the possibility of holding another major event in Winnipeg, the city looked south, to the Americas.

The 1999 Pan Am Games were a culmination of a dream that began in 1987, with a vision that Winnipeg could repeat its centennial year success story. Don MacKenzie, the head of the Manitoba Sports Federation at that time, took a small contingent to Indianapolis to appraise the 1987 Pan American Games. He fell in love with the Games all over again.

Four years later, on the heels of a very successful 1990 Western Canada Summer Games, Winnipeg City Council overwhelmingly approved a motion to support a bid to return the Pan American Games to Winnipeg in 1999. In April 1991, Winnipeg Mayor Bill Norrie beckoned MacKenzie and Barbara Huck, a former sports writer, to co-chair the bid process. With the assistance of a dedicated board of directors, an inexhaustible committee that represented a broad cross-section of the Winnipeg business, sports and cultural community, and support from the City and Province, the Winnipeg Bid Committee went to work. Premier Gary Filmon was brought aboard to assist in the bid to win the Canadian rights to pursue the Games. The competition was formidable: Halifax, with its east coast appeal; Toronto, which had just lost a bid for the 1996 Olympics; Edmonton, which had staged a very successful Commonwealth and World Student Games; and Sherbrooke, Quebec, representing an influential province which had not had a major games since the Olympics in 1976.

Twenty months and thousands of hours of effort later, the Winnipeg team presented its Games plan to the Canadian Olympic Association's Board of Directors in Toronto on December 5, 1992. The decision went to three ballots before Winnipeg was selected by a one-vote majority over Toronto. The international bid process lay ahead.

The first task at hand was the preparation necessary to convince the 42 nations of the Pan American Sports Organization (PASO) that Winnipeg was the best place to stage the 1999 Games. With the assistance of the Canadian Olympic Association and the three levels of government, the committee rolled out the red carpet for the PASO delegates to visit Friendly Manitoba, and in turn made a series of visits to nations of the Americas to win their hearts.

VOLUNTEERS

The Pan Am Games, particularly in North America, had suffered diminution since the 1987 Games in Indianapolis. There was very little media coverage in 1991 in Cuba and in 1995 in Argentina. PASO needed to get North America - be it the Americans or Canadians - back involved in a significant way. "They knew we would do a good job and they needed a first-rate set of Games," MacKenzie assured. But he also knew that Winnipeg's greatest strength was also its greatest weakness. It was unusual to have a city host twice, and only 32 years apart. But PASO directors remembered the spirit of the '67 Games; Winnipeg could once again rekindle that enthusiasm for the Games.

MacKenzie recalled PASO asking the question, "Why Winnipeg again ... such a big beautiful country, why not another city?" MacKenzie remembered the answer: "Because we have the greatest volunteers anywhere." It was that community spirit upon which the committee built its proposal. A different philosophy or approach to get the Games was needed. Being the best was not necessarily going to work. Winnipeg had to be more than that, said MacKenzie. The city promised that its community spirit would raise the bar for Games for the new millennium.

In July 1994, a delegation of nearly 40 Manitobans landed in Guayaquil, Ecuador, the site of the final selection process. As it had been in Toronto nearly two years earlier, the competition was fierce, led by the Dominican Republic city of Santo Domingo and Columbia's Bogota. Once again, it took three ballots to decide the eventual winner. Bogota was eliminated on the first ballot, the second was a 25-25 tie, and it was only on a tie-breaking third ballot that PASO President Mario Vazquez Rana announced Winnipeg the winner by 28 votes to 22. "My heart stopped," confessed Winnipeg's new mayor, Susan Thompson. The rest is now history.

Enter Sandy Riley, a 1976 Olympic sailor, and newly appointed CEO of Investors Group, headquartered on Portage Avenue in Winnipeg. He had had some involvement with the Winnipeg Bid Committee as chair of a corporate initiative committee. Mayor Thompson was charged with striking an organizing committee - the Pan American Games Society. She immediately sought out Riley as its chairman. He hired MacKenzie as its Chief Executive Officer.

The XIII Pan American Games were an undeniable success. Despite certain elements of negativity within the community prior to the Games from those who Riley described as "looking at challenges before opportunities", even the organizing committee itself was overwhelmed by the enormity and near-flawnessness of their offering. In a flurry of statistical grandeur, Riley reported that over one million people participated in the Games across all facets, equivalent to the population of the entire province of Manitoba and comparable to the hosting of two Grey Cups a day for seventeen straight days.

The Games Society set out to accomplish three key objectives in the hosting of the event. A volunteer-delivered Games was paramount. Organizers wanted to run an event that the athletes who came from around the Americas would remember for the rest of their lives. And finally, they were intent on showcasing Winnipeg and Canada to the Americas and in doing so, revitalize community pride and spirit in the City of Winnipeg. "We've done it as well as any

Dan Galbraith

community could possibly have done it," Riley concluded. "We wanted to show the Americas that this is a community on its toes, not on its heels."

MacKenzie felt that a major factor in the success of the Games was keeping things simple. "We had to with our tight budget," he explained. "Our Games were twice the size of Victoria's Commonwealth Games, but our budget was 10 to 15 million dollars less. We had to be creative." When Bob McMahon, the Games Chief Operating Officer, speaks about the budget, he speaks about balance. "We strived for balance and we found it. We'll be asked why our Games were successful and it may be a disservice to other games organizers to provide an answer. Whatever the answer is, it worked in Winnipeg, but there is no cookie-cutter approach to an event like this." He equated the financial aspect of the Games to a four-legged stool where government funding, sponsorship revenue, and public support such as ticket sales, still need a prudent host society as the last leg to keep the bench upright.

But when the key factor to the Games' success comes into question, there was no disagreement between the chief administrator and the chief operator. "The Games were blessed by the spirit of the people of the community," MacKenzie asserted. "The volunteers delivered the Games," he said in deference to the 20,000-member union. "Winnipeg can be slow to come to the table, but they come through. They'll be there when needed."

VOLUNTEERS

Keith Levit

THE CORPORATE FOUNDATION

The bar was set at $23.5 million. But the Host Society's Sponsorship Program kept jumping higher, reaching a final height of $28 million in corporate support for the 1999 Pan Am Games. Four levels of commitment - ranging from $200,000 to $4 million - were procured from international, national and provincial organizations. But the bucks did not stop there. Diane Lloyd, General Manager of the Pan American Games Society's Sponsorship Division estimated that collectively, another $10 million were spent by the sponsors to leverage their initial sponsorship pledges. From banners and billboards around the city to magazine advertising and corporate T-shirts, corporate involvement was ubiquitous. Lloyd commented that one of her greatest challenges within the sponsorship program was balancing the enthusiasm from non-sponsors with the rights and benefits of her paying corporate customers where the use of official Pan Am marks was concerned. "We didn't want to discourage Winnipeg businesses from showing their support of the athletes in their store fronts, but sponsors' rights had to be protected too."

Manitoba Telecom Services (MTS) was the first corporation to commit to Winnipeg's Games. They were joined later by three other Official Partners - the highest level of sponsorship next to the three government Funding Partners - which included Panasonic, Swatch and The Document Company - Xerox, all of which made major contributions to the infrastructure of the Games. The governments' contributions to the $140 million Games budget included $10 million from the city, $42.5 million from the province and $49 million from Ottawa.

"We signed on in 1996 as the Games' first partner and it was a lonely year waiting for others," noted Wayne Wilson, MTS's Executive Director. MTS provided four levels of service at the Games: local or "dial-tone", wireless (cellular and private two-way radios), the broadcast network carrying signals from each venue to the host broadcaster which in turn sent them out throughout the world, and the data network which included results, accreditation, medical information and so on.

Timing is everything at any set of games, and the Pan Ams were no exception. Before the 5,000 athletes arrived for the Games, Winnipeg was wired. Swatch, the "Official Timekeeper of the Games", and its miles of cable, tonnes of state-of-the-art timekeeping equipment and teams of professional engineers, landed weeks earlier. "Timekeeping is no different than any other event you would witness at games," said Peter Hurzler, Vice-President of Marketing at Swatch Timing and the man in charge of the Winnipeg operations. "To be the best, our team has spent years training. We design new equipment using the latest breakthroughs in technology. We constantly refine each nuance of our technique. We're always pushing to do it faster and better." Swatch counted on 19 tonnes of timekeeping equipment in Winnipeg, valued at $2,528,325 (Cdn.), and 50 timekeeping professionals brought in from seven countries.

The Swatch Timing team was also responsible for the data handling at the venues which included providing printouts of results, start lists, competition statistics, television graphics and the commentator information system. Winnipeg's tie to Swatch dates back to the 1967 Pan Am Games when Swiss Timing, a Swatch Group division, served as the official timekeeper. The 1967 Games boasted a number of technological breakthroughs including the use of touch pads for swimming events.

Xerox also played a major role in the dissemination of information at the Games. As the name sponsor of the Xerox Main Press Centre, the company was responsible for ensuring that the world's press that had descended on Winnipeg was well served, and in turn, the Games well presented. Marlene Smart, Xerox's Pan Am Games Project Manager emphasized that the company has a long history of commitment to Canadian

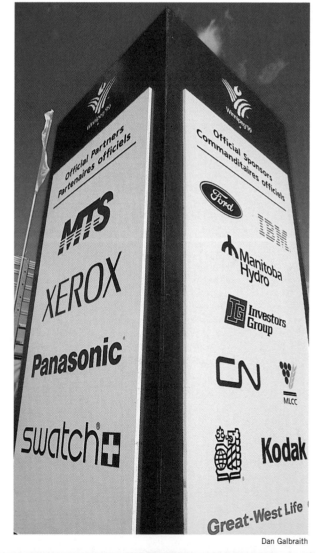

Dan Galbraith

VOLUNTEERS

sports. During her involvement with the Games, Smart was most impressed with the sense of pride that built among partners and sponsors. "We're a smaller city so we had to really pool our skills and build these Games together," she related. "But we were mature in recognizing when we didn't have the human resources in Winnipeg for a particular aspect of the development and operations of the Games and then we sought outside help," she qualified. The success of the Games, she felt, was hinged on the willingness of everyone involved, the Host Society included, to pull together to ensure that it was a good event for all, sponsors as well.

Panasonic joined the sponsorship team in 1998 with a commitment to provide a large range of equipment to the Games including digital component camcorders, security and surveillance equipment, and Astrovision Large Screen Video Display Systems. Panasonic also provided colour monitors and receivers in certain Pan Am venues. Tomas Murakami, President of Panasonic Canada Inc., was very enthusiastic about the partnership from the start. "Panasonic is a world leader in equipment and systems integration, and the Pan American Games will be a showcase event to high-

Dan Galbraith

light our capabilities in video production, presentation and security applications," said Murakami after the sponsorship signing. "Events like the Pan American Games allow us to use our equipment in the most demanding situations, live and with the world watching."

Despite being a worldwide sponsor of the Olympics since 1988, the 1999 Pan Am Games was the first time Panasonic was involved in an event of this magnitude in Canada. Ian Kilvert, Panasonic Canada's Director of Corporate Communications, explained that 40 per cent of the company's business is on the industrial side - business to business - for which the Pan Ams offered an opportunity to expose their broadcast equipment. "We've been well known on the consumer side for 30 years, but the general public isn't aware of our revolutionary contributions to the broadcast industry," he remarked.

Panasonic worked closely with the Canadian Broadcasting Corporation (CBC) in Winnipeg, playing a prominent role during the Games in the operations of the Panasonic International Broadcast Centre located in

"I volunteered because I wanted to do something for my province and my city. Seeing how this community came togth the spirit, and how big these Games were, have to be my most memorable experiences." *Nina Ardie, Media Servic*

the downtown Winnipeg CBC building. Security and surveillance cameras and equipment in the athlete villages, large screen video display technology (Astrovision) at key venues like The Forks, Winnipeg Stadium and the University of Manitoba Stadium, coupled with their industrial audio equipment, or RAMSA, for public address systems made up the lion's share of Panasonic product at the Games. And of course, a few televisions in and around athlete and hospitality lounges were not overlooked.

Keith Levit

One of Kilvert's most memorable moments at the Games came on the morning after the men's 100-metre final at the track. The Winnipeg Free Press featured the winner on the cover of their daily *Pan Am Special* section. The U.S. athlete was captured flying across the finish line, arms wide-spread with Panasonic emblazoned across his chest. Panasonic received athlete bib presence for all men's athletic events. "Seeing our name on the front page of the Free Press was an added bonus." Not to mention a gratifying homecoming for the displaced Winnipegger who still refers to the city as his hometown.

Fabulous imagery and compelling stories in the newspaper were all in a day's work for the Winnipeg Free Press - 18 days work to be exact, including its keepsake wrap-up special Pan Am Section. "Joining the Games as a Proud Supporter was a natural for us," said Laurie Finley, Director of Advertising Sales & Marketing for the daily newspaper. "The Winnipeg Free Press has been part of the community since the incorporation of the city," he added. Each day of the Games, the Pan Am community and the community of Winnipeg at large, clamored to the special section for Pan Am news, highlights, results, photography and the inside scoop on the athletes, volunteers and organizers. Collector's items they were, for locals and visitors alike.

Among the group of seven Official Sponsors of the Games, notable contributions were made by them all. The Investors Group, with its head office in Winnipeg, built their sponsorship around their theme of "Looking back at the '67 Games ... Looking forward to the '99 Games" and supported it with banners and super-billboards around the city. An inspiring mural was commissioned for above their Portage Avenue front doors. Richard Irish, Vice-President of Corporate and Community Affairs for Investors Group, admitted that he was overwhelmed by the way the community took to the Games. "The extraordinarily positive feeling in the city was a great byproduct of the event, particularly

VOLUNTEERS

Don Gaudette

because Winnipeggers have a tendency to be hard on ourselves," he revealed. "We've shown we're equal to the task."

Great-West Life, another early sponsor, felt a real sense of responsibility to support the Pan Am Games because it was such a huge community initiative. The company helped raise awareness of the Games through an immense banner on the side of its building, and co-ordinated several projects for its employees, including a sports display highlighting the company's involvement with the '67 Games, Pan Am-themed luncheons, and contests and special incentives for families and children.

Janet Belanger, Manager of Community Relations for Great-West, said the company's Pan Am support was a natural fit, following its involvement with the '67 Games and its generous history of funding community events across Canada. "Great-West has been a part of this community for more than 100 years, and we're proud of the commitment Winnipeg volunteers put forward in showcasing the best this city has to offer. The spirit of the city really made these Games 'golden,'" Belanger remarked. "We saw the spirit in Winnipeggers during the 1997 flood ... it was great to see that same spirit as part of a very positive event," she said.

Manitoba Hydro, a staunch supporter of numerous cultural and charitable events across the province, positioned itselfs as "The Power Behind the Games." Linda McCullough, Manager of Business Communications, remarked that the slogan could mean a number of things, but that it essentially meant the people behind the Games - the volunteers. Over 400 Manitoba Hydro employees contributed their own time as volunteers at the Games. In addition to that, the crown company put together a 300-member clean-up crew to service the venues. Not surprisingly, Manitoba Hydro sponsored a "Volunteer Guide" for all volunteers as an incremental package to their original contribution. "These Games won't be a here-today-gone-tomorrow event," McCullough declared. "There will be a long-lasting impact on the community."

Another striking contribution came from Winnipeg's Ford dealers, spearheaded by Bob Kozminski, President of Keystone Ford. Kozminski knew early on that Ford Motor Company, nationally, had to get involved in the Games. What the Games required in the way of vehicles was too big for the local dealers. Kozminski brought the automotive giant aboard with a $2 million cost-basis commitment. Fifty Pan Am vehicles were on the road over the course of the two years leading up to the Games; 800 vehicles during Games-time. Not only that, Kozminski assisted in getting Manitoba Public Insurance to provide $250,000 worth of insurance on the vehicles. Kozminski claimed that the logistics involved in amassing the vehicles - licensing, cleaning, delivering, inspections - may have been his greatest challenge. "Nonetheless," he reflected, "it was important for us to give something back to the community. We felt that it was important to get on board early to give the sponsorship program at shot in the arm."

The Games' sponsorship program also relied heavily on Official Suppliers, one of which was Sportec, a sports information technology company contracted to provide the results and information systems for the Games. Based in Spain, Sportec provided the most advanced computer technology software for the competition control, results management and distribution to all the end users (CBC-TV, journalists, commentators, spectators). Commentator Information Systems, and the Info '99 System (con-

Dan Galbraith

VOLUNTEERS

taining results and other relevant Games information in three languages). A team of 58 Sportec staff worked very closely with the sports and technology organizers to customize the software programs to specifically suit the rules, requirements and regulations of the 41 sports of the XIIIth Pan Am Games. Sportec worked closely with the CBC to accommodate their graphics needs through the use of Sportec's televisiongraphics generator, AGILE (Animated Graphic Interface for Live Events). This system provided animated graphics for eight of the televised sports: athletics, baseball, softball, basketball, soccer, volleyball, beach volleyball and weightlifting. Sportec offers their computer services around the world - the Asian Games in Bangkok and the World University Games in Mallorca, Spain in 1999 as well.

The sponsorship component of the Games was augmented with support from Winnipeg's local businesses through a program called Friends of the Games. Nearly 200 local companies contributed anywhere from $5,000 to $150,000 across several levels of involvement. The Friends of the Games target revenue was established at $2.5 million but came to rest soundly at more than $4 million.

Ken Gigliott

VOLUNTEERS

THE LOOK OF THE GAMES

Resistance was futile. Upon arriving in Winnipeg during the Pan Am Games it was impossible to ignore the bombardment of billboards, banners decorating large corporate towers and merchandise that had taken over as Pan A'mania began its hypnotic hold over the city. At the heart of it all was the work of Palmer Jarvis DDB. Their creation of a simple design of rough lines enhanced through bright, energetic colours became the symbol of the XIIIth Pan American Games - the logo or "tattoo" that ensured the object in question was officially endorsed by the Pan Am Games Society.

Palmer Jarvis DDB won the rights to produce the Games marks through an open contest for design firms in the province of Manitoba. In the end, two designers were selected. Kevin Braun had his Games logo selected, and Ron Sawchuk had his sport icons chosen. Merging the two designers' work, the final submission was accepted by a Pan Am Games selection committee. "The contest was open to the entire design community here in Manitoba ... it was really something that the decision was narrowed down to two guys working in the same place," commented Sawchuk.

Using the 1967 logo as a launching point, Braun wanted to focus on the athletes while giving a sense of place for the Games. Staying away from geometric lines and incorporating new dynamic colours, the new logo was symbolic to the Games and to the city. "The logo was meant to be an evolution of the logo from 1967," explained Sawchuk. "It was also meant to place Winnipeg geographically. The forms coming from the left and right are meant to represent the Red and Assiniboine Rivers. The colours are meant to symbolize the different cultures of Winnipeg and also the cultures of the Americas. The yellow-orange head is representative of the setting sun on the Prairies." Another interpretation depicts a stylized athlete, arms raised in jubilation. Braun used both interpretations to develop the logo.

The sport icons were modeled after prehistoric rock drawings that were discovered in the Canadian Shield. Using these artifacts as inspiration gave Sawchuk the opportunity to pay tribute to Manitoba's Aboriginal heritage. "The sport icons are very true to those original drawings," Sawchuk revealed. "I executed them with brushwork to give a very rough look, like they had been painted on rock. The organic lines in the logo were meant to have synergy with the sport icons. That's one of the things

Dan Galbraith

VOLUNTEERS

Dan Galbraith

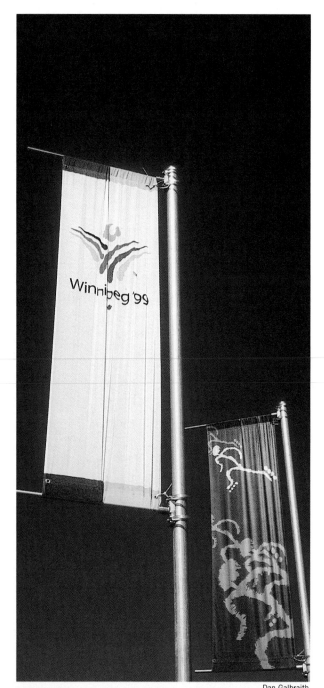

Dan Galbraith

we finessed after we discovered the Games Society wanted to combine our submissions into one look."

Another Palmer Jarvis DDB project was the commercials that announced the arrival of the Games. The dramatic commercials depicted athletes competing with their traditional playing fields exchanged for geographically significant landmarks from the area. These images were also printed as posters, and handed out at the various information kiosks that proliferated the competition sites. There were four images: a swimmer gliding over glowing fields of wheat, a volleyball player spiking over the Lockport bridge, a high jumper leaping over the facade at St. Boniface, and a discus thrower high atop the Manitoba Legislature. (The perch of Winnipeg's Golden Boy.) The commercials were a huge success. Kudos came from the design community as well as the general population and the sheer abundance of temporarily tattooed spectators (both young and old) at any given event attested to the lengths to which the Games community had embraced the logo and icons.

VOLUNTEERS

"I've met so many new people and made new friends. I'm proud of Winnipeg and wanted to make sure the visitors had a good impression." *Annette Boucha*

MUCHACHOS

An outreach program designed to enhance awareness of the XIII Pan American Games was launched a full year before the Games began. The Muchachos Panamericanos visited parades, fairs, festivals, sporting and special events in Winnipeg and targeted communities within a 560 kilometre radius of the city to provide the public with ticket and general information about the Pan Ams.

The on-the-road corps of ambassadors was comprised of 14 university students who traveled in teams of two in brightly coloured Ford-sponsored vans. Two crews were based in Winnipeg, but the Muchachos ventured as far as Saskatchewan, Ontario, North Dakota and Minnesota to participate in local activities and special promotional events.

In addition to distributing ticket information and generating enthusiasm for the 42-nation sporting and cultural event, the Muchachos distributed volunteer forms, Home Stay information, and responded to general public inquiries. Pan Am mascots, Pato Panamericano and Lorita Panamericana frequently toured with the Muchachos caravan. "I can't think of a better summer job," guaranteed Muchacha Karen Alho.

VOLUNTEERS

A sporting event of this magnitude is indisputably about people coming together to celebrate. Winnipeg and its neighbouring communities served up a celebration of sport, friendship, competition and culture for the city, province and country, as well as for all of the Americas - a dynamic festival of life, dreams and aspirations.

SPIRIT OF SPORT

LET THE GAMES BEGIN

Emotions were running high and the heat was on for Pan Am Games organizers to dazzle a crowd of 40,000 spectators at Winnipeg Stadium and the millions of others around the world watching. Winnipeg, affectionately referred to as "the heart of the continent", lived up to its reputation of being a proud and spirited city.

Despite the unusually hot and humid evening temperatures, when the clock struck eight and the Winnipeg Symphony Orchestra played its first note the heat was forgotten and a curious crowd settled in for more than two hours of spectacular entertainment.

Don Gaudette

The show opened with a lone performer taking flight across the stadium floor. Disguised in an earthy-green costume, he held a larger-than-life puppet goose over his head in search of a place to land. A flock of nearly 200 just like him soon followed. When the fabricated geese came to rest, Canada's distinctive birds harmoniously formed Winnipeg's Pan Am Games logo.

Then the athletes, more than 5,000 of them, marched into the stadium - each team proudly brandishing their respective flags. The 42 participating nations arrived in alphabetical order with the exception of Argentina, the previous Pan Am Games host first, and Canada last, a tradition for the current host country. The crowd went wild at first sight of the red and white flag peeking out the entrance of the holding tent (where the athletes waited their turn to enter). The crowd roar was deafening as the spectators rose to their feet collectively to salute Canada's flag bearer and Winnipeg's own, Tanya

VOLUNTEERS

Norm Lourenco

Dubnicoff. A sea of Canadian flags waved to the athletes from the stands thanks to Ceremony organizers who thoughtfully provided each seat with a booklet of the flags of all the participating Pan American nations. The mini flags enabled the audience to participate in the ceremony, and pay tribute to each nation as it paraded through the stadium.

One could not have imagined that the crowd could get any louder, but it did. When the men's water polo team sprinted around the field carrying the Canadian flag for all to see, Winnipeg Stadium erupted again. The spirited athletes left their informal formation amongst the enormous Canadian contingent and ran wildly stirring unimaginable emotion and patriotism within the hearts of the inspired onlookers.

The tradition of having the athletes enter the stadium at the start of the Ceremony which enables them to see the entire show is very Canadian. The Calgary Games

Don Gaudette

VOLUNTEERS

Don Gaudette

in 1988 were the first Olympics to follow this athlete-friendly format; Victoria's Commonwealth Games were the first to do so as well.

After the spectacular entrance of all the competitors, a colourful mix of music, dance and tradition that makes Winnipeg unique, swept spectators off their feet. The field was alive with dancing colour. "We worked to capture one of Winnipeg's strengths: something it is known for across the country is its richness of cultural life, from culture rooted in folkloric traditions to the classical arts," described Larry Desrochers, producer and director of the Opening and Closing Ceremonies.

There were three main production numbers: "Heart of the Continent," which depicted the four distinct seasons of Manitoba, "Go For Gold," which told the story of a young girl striving to be a champion and "City of the Plains," the compelling story of the people who built the City of Winnipeg. These performances flooded Winnipeg Stadium with the brilliantly choreographed movement and breathtaking costumes of 3,400 performers, including 500 cultural dancers and a magical gospel choir of nearly 300.

Members of the First Nations community created 42 Star Blankets in the colours of each country's flag and presented them to the nation's respective team leader as part of the festivities. There were eight additional blankets made in the Pan Am colours and those were presented to the dignitaries in attendance, including Princess Anne. The giving of Star Blankets is a tradition within First Nations communities. Recipients are only presented with the symbolic blanket on special occasions. It is considered a token of respect to give one, and a tremendous honour to receive it.

The symbolic showcasing of Canadian history continued, represented by fifty Royal Canadian Mounted Police dressed in the traditional red uniforms and wide rimmed hats, marching onto the field two by two. Halted by their vociferous leader and instructed to divide, the stadium again burst with excitement when an enormous Canadian flag was unfurled between the two rows of men and women.

Canadian pride overtly filled the air. With glowing hearts, the national anthem was received. With the RCMP still clutching the flag, the last note of O' Canada was followed by a thunderous blare from above the stadium as the Canadian Armed Forces' Snowbirds, with impeccable timing, rocketed in formation directly overhead without warning.

Don Gaudette

Once settled back in their seats, Princess Anne addressed a captivated crowd with the story of how her father officially opened the 1967 Pan Am Games in Winnipeg. "I remember when my father stood here 32 years ago. I remember the elegance of the Opening Ceremony, the same as I see here tonight. However, the most striking difference I do notice," she said with a pause to set up an amusing story ending, "is that it is not raining tonight." The audience responded with respectful laughter. In 1967, pouring rain arrived as an uninvited guest to the Opening Ceremony and refused to leave. Princess Anne then acknowledged all those who organized the Games and the enormous challenge they embraced. "This is my third visit to Manitoba and I am very excited to see some of the events over the next few days. This is an extraordinary time for those who participate in these Games and I hope all of you reach your goals and make your dreams a reality," she concluded.

Norm Lourenco

VOLUNTEERS

Mr. Sandy Riley, chairman of the Games board, took to the podium next with a touching message: "I have a special word to all the athletes; do your very best, have a great time and may the friendships and memories of the XIIIth Pan Am Games last a lifetime."

Perhaps the most unexpected moment of the Opening Ceremony came when the president of the Pan American Sports Organization, Mario Vazquez Rana, had to pause during his speech as it was interrupted by the "wave" cheer that deliberately circled the stadium four times before it subsided. Rana stood silent and in awe as he watched spectators, athletes and even the yellow-clad choir join in the revolving excitement.

As the ceremony moved on through the evening, Governor General Romeo LeBlanc was called upon to declare the Games open. The Athletes' Oath followed, read by Winnipeg racquetball competitor Sherman Greenfeld and badminton player Denyse Julien. They, on behalf of all athletes, promised to compete in fairness and in the pursuit of excellence.

Darkness had now fallen over the prairie sky and at last it was time for the lighting of the cauldron, signifying the official start to the Games. The suspense mounted. Who would carry the torch to its final destination?

Organizers courageously attended to an unfinished matter. Seven of the ten aboriginal torch runners who brought the Pan Am flame to Winnipeg in 1967, but not to the cauldron, were asked to finish their mission. They were provided with the honour of carrying the Pan Am Torch into the stadium exactly 32 years later, to the day. Three giant canoes rolled on to the field with crisp blue

Don Gaudette

Norm Lourenco

banners enveloping both sides of each to simulate sparkling blue water. The best kept secrets of the ceremony were to follow - the final torch bearer and the torch lighters. The lead canoe passed the flame to Ida Whitford, a 12-year-old Ojibway from Sandy Bay First Nations Reserve. Voted top female athlete at the 1999 Indigenous Games, Ida was bestowed the honour of escorting the well-traveled torch across the stadium floor for one last hand-off.

The torch was handed to Alwyn Morris, an Aboriginal Quebecer, who won double gold in canoeing and kayaking at the 1984 Los Angeles Olympics and to Silken Laumann, the rower who won Canada's heart with a bronze-medal performance at the 1992 Barcelona Olympics, in spite of a badly broken leg. Both raised the torch toward the crowd and headed for the tower. They galloped up the stairs as drums beat loudly and the choir chanted traditional aboriginal songs. It was sheer delight; this was the

Don Gaudette

| 43

VOLUNTEERS

Don Gaudette

moment Manitoba was waiting for. The torch was positioned directly behind and above the athlete seating. There they were, in their nation's colours, their dreams intact. The torch was hoisted to the giant cauldron and with a boom the Games were ignited. Fireworks decorated the sky. Let the Games begin.

The energy that flowed through Winnipeg Stadium that night was breathtaking and inspiring. The people of Winnipeg and across Manitoba represented their country with pride and dignity. They rose to the challenge. In hosting the XIIIth Pan American Games, Winnipeg created something it already prides itself upon. History. And Manitoba demonstrated to the Americas that spirit and pride are alive in Canada.

VOLUNTEERS

Dan Galbraith

WINNIPEG'S GOLDEN GIRL

She could have been the poster girl for the 1999 Pan American Games. Winnipeg native Tanya Dubnicoff performed like a gold medallist on and off the cycling track. Winnipeg Mayor Glen Murray paid her tribute appropriately: "She has breathed more life and excitement into these Games than any other individual."

It all began when she was selected to carry the Canadian flag into Winnipeg Stadium during the Opening Ceremony. One would wonder what kind of pressure is associated with being appointed to lead your country's team. "It was unreal; it was such a rush," Dubnicoff beamed. "I just felt so excited, it's hard to describe. I was so happy and so emotional." Dubnicoff laughed off the suggestion that she may have missed out on some of the celebrating amongst her teammates behind her while walking ahead of the entire Canadian contingent. "No way, I like being out in front," she quipped.

"Carrying the flag and just being associated with Canada brings so much pride; it's just unbelievable." It was a very touching moment as Dubnicoff made her way around the field displaying Canada's flag and desperately searching the audience for her parents. "That was the

ON THE EVE OF THE MUCH-ANTICIPATED OPENING CEREMONY, AND TO THE APPROVING APPLAUSE OF HER FELLOW ATHLETES, TANYA DUBNICOFF PROUDLY RECEIVED THE CANADIAN FLAG AT HISTORIC FORT GIBRALTOR IN ST. BONIFACE. CHOSEN TO LEAD HER COUNTRY INTO WINNIPEG STADIUM AS FLAG BEARER, THE 29-YEAR-OLD TWO-TIME PAN AM GOLD MEDALLIST WAS NEAR TEARS. "I AM DEFINITELY HONOURED TO BE CHOSEN," SHE ASSURED. "I WANT TO HONOUR ALL OF YOU AT THE OPENING CEREMONY. I HAVE PRIDE AS A CANADIAN AND PRIDE AS AN ATHLETE TO DO THE BEST JOB I POSSIBLY CAN."

VOLUNTEERS

Don Gaudette

Dan Galbraith

moment I had been waiting for. I had a CBC microphone attached to my jacket and I mentioned out loud that I was looking for my parents. As soon as I said it the production people had a camera on my family in the stands and I could see them on the big screen." Dubnicoff smiled, "I was a mess after that, many emotions came rushing over me. I'll never forget it."

Being a member of the Canadian Team and carrying the flag was a dream come true for Dubnicoff. "*That* [carrying the flag] was my Pan Am Games - the ultimate dream of mine. I was excited about racing but holding the flag was what I was waiting for." Dubnicoff confessed that it was very nerve-wracking waiting with the Canadian Team in the tent before the Ceremony's athlete parade. "I knew the crowd was going to go crazy. The anticipation was killing me." Dubnicoff admitted the feeling was even more nail-biting than waiting at a starting line. "Competing for me isn't pressure, it is rising to the occasion. There's no need to be stressed when I've done the work. When I've trained hard it is my time to shine." And shine she did.

Norm Lourenco

A HISTORICAL JOURNEY

Beginning its voyage on June 23rd, 1999 near Mexico City, the official symbol of the XIIIth Pan American Games traveled nearly 17,000 kilometres by canoe, bicycle, air, rail and foot, and through three countries before it was paraded into Winnipeg Stadium on Friday, July 23rd to signify the opening of the Games. Sponsored by Canadian National Railway, the torch made stops in 20 Manitoba communities helping to ignite more excitement for Winnipeg's Games.

But even before its traditional last-leg run into Winnipeg Stadium, the torch's lengthy journey was already steeped in symbolism. Traveling Winnipeg's Perimeter Highway by a cycle relay the torch was then passed to a 99-person relay which in turn presented it to Gary Filmon, the Premier of Manitoba, at the "Taste of Manitoba" celebration. In conjunction with Winnipeg's pre-Games Mardi Gras Street Festival, the flame was then yielded to Mayor Glen Murray in Market Square. Moving to the Winnipeg Legislative Building, the torch was ceremoniously furnished to the First Nations Tribal Journey by an assembly of Metis, after a moment of silence in front of the Louis Riel Memorial. Riel, a

47

VOLUNTEERS

Metis, was instrumental in drafting Manitoba's Bill of Rights which facilitated Manitoba's official status as Canada's 5th province in 1870.

In the backyard of the Legislature grounds on the shore of the Red, the torch took to the river. Carried by a proud Billy Jack Grieves, the youngest member of the Tribal Journey, the torch was en route to its temporary display at the Oodena Bowl at the Forks. The flame rested at this historical meeting place at the junction of the Assiniboine and Red Rivers for half a day, as it awaited its final ceremonious duty - lighting of the cauldron at Winnipeg Stadium to let the Games begin.

Both the federal and provincial governments were on hand for the Torch Run's conclusion in support of the heritage, culture and spirit that it exemplified. "As Canada prepares to open its arms to representatives of 42 countries we are also ensuring the Aboriginal community has a prominent role in the extraordinary cultural celebrations that will characterize these Games," said Foreign Affairs Minister Lloyd Axworthy. "The Tribal Journey and Cultural Village at the Forks further enrich the Pan Am experience for the Aboriginal community and all visitors to Winnipeg."

Greeted by a modest group of onlookers along the riverbank the torch, held high by Grieves, arrived to the drums of the Pimicikamak Cree Nation beating out a welcoming song. The flame was brought to the Oodena Bowl and lowered to light a temporary cauldron, much to the pleasure of those on hand who may have been taking advantage of their only opportunity to get a firsthand look at the legendary Pan Am torch.

Norm Lourenco

VOLUNTEERS

VIA PITTNER • GORD PIZEY • LAURYN PIZEY - ALLEN • SHELAGH PIZEY - ALLEN • SHARON PLAITIN • JANIS PLATTS • CATHY PLESKACH • CATHY PLESKACH • JEANETTE PLETT • YVONNE PLISCHKE • TARA PODAIMA • TARA POINTKOSKI • MELISSA POIRIER • EMIL POKLAR • MICKEY POKLAR • KATHLEEN POLEY • SHAYNA POLLOCK • STEPHANIE POLLOCK • JACKIE POLLON • TAMARA POMANSKI • TANYA POMANSKI • JHOLEEN PONCE • DENNIS PONTE • CHRISTIE LEE PONTES • LUCY PONTES - BOTELHO • KATELYNN POOLE • CRYSTAL POPADYNETZ • CHELSEA POROZNUK • CASSANDRA PORPIGLIA • CHRISTINE PORPIGLIA • SHAWN PORTEOUS • DAVID PORTER • KELSEY PORTER • SARA PORTER • RACHEL POSNER • GINETTE POULIN • DAYTON POWELL • VALRIE POWELL • CARMEN POWERS • HUGUETTE POWLESLAND • ALINA POWORZNIK • BOYCEE PRESINGULAR • DONNA PRESINGULAR • HEIDI PRESINGULAR • JINGO PRESINGULAR • MAX PRESSMAN • MICHAEL PREZA • GEORGE PRICE • SHANDIS PRICE • AARON PRIDHAM

• HAILEY PROCYSH
TANIS PRODUNIUK •
BIE PROKOPCHUK •
KA PROKOSH • ELIZA
PROSKURNIK • CHE

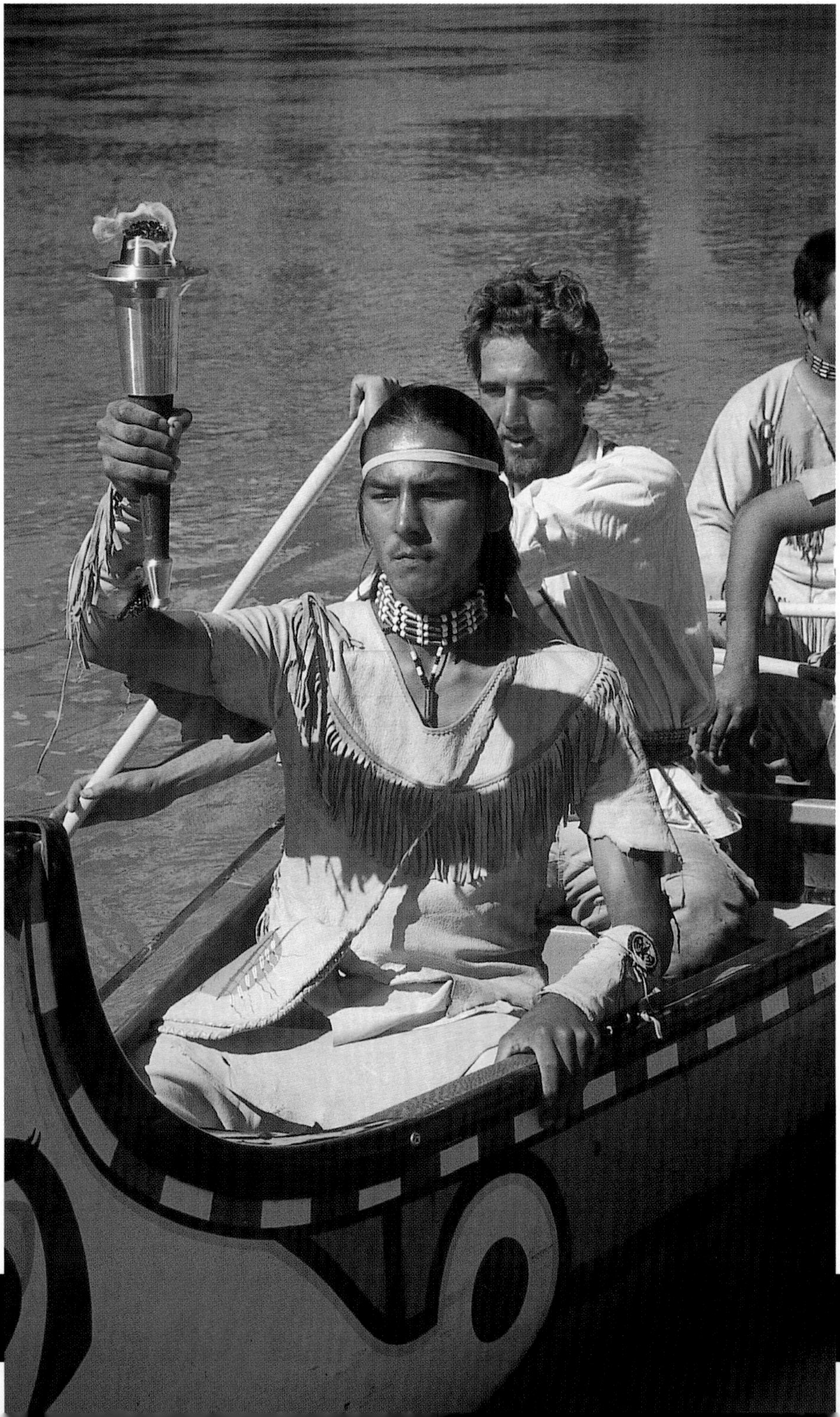

Honoured to have carried the torch down the Red River, Grieves' eyes gave way to his emotions. "I'm leaving a legacy for my children and the Native people across the Americas," he professed. "I'm overwhelmed. The adrenaline is still running through my body strong."

A relay team of twelve runners, representing the twelve former host cities of the Pan Am Games propelled the torch on its evening journey from the Oodena Bowl to Winnipeg Stadium's Opening Ceremony which as filled to capacity with an unflagging crowd anticipating its arrival. Thirty-two years after Winnipeg's inaugural Pan Am Games, seven of the ten original torch runners from the 1967 Pan Am Games were honoured guests at the Opening Ceremony, important players in the part of the torch's approach to the cauldron. Thirty-two years to the day, seven men finished what ten were disappointingly not empowered to do in 1967. Riding high in three over-sized motorized canoes, their mission was finally served. The torch had arrived.

was a volunteer in 1967 as a phys. ed. student, you just can't compare the two except for the spirit. There weren't hlete villages or the technology that there is today, but there was the same community spirit." *Judy Moon*

VOLUNTEERS

Norm Lourenco

THE HEARTBEAT OF AMERICA'S GAMES

Winnipeg's Pan Am Games Society knew how to bring people together. As recruitment manager in the Society's volunteer division, Susan Shortill-Lopez helped to gather up 18,575 volunteers for the Games. And that doesn't include the 3,000 volunteers involved with the Opening and Closing Ceremony, or Manitoba Hydro's Clean Team of 300 that ensured clean venues. "We were amazed at the response we received right off the bat," Shortill-Lopez remarked. "They came out in droves."

Heading up the Recruitment Committee Shortill-Lopez, of Winnipeg, began their campaign for the Pan Am Games Society two years before the Games began. She admitted it was a little stressful at first. The number of volunteers that were needed to make sure the Games ran smoothly was daunting. But the enthusiasm from the community quickly put her at ease. "We were overjoyed with our success in filling all the positions."

There were three different levels of training that volunteers attended, depending on their position, before they took their posts. The first level was "general training" and basically focused on the history and basic details of the Games. A second level was "specific training" geared for those in positions involving protocol or security. The third level was "venue training" which taught volunteers about the physical layout of each venue and information pertaining to the management of visitors to that venue.

Shortill-Lopez was astonished that people of all ages were interested in volunteering at the event. Approximately 2,500 volunteers were between the ages of 55 and

VOLUN

65, and over 1,000 were 65 years of age or older. There were also "games groupies" - fervent devotees who follow big sporting events around the globe as volunteer participants. "We had volunteers from across Canada - from Newfoundland to the Yukon - from as far away as Florida in the U.S., from Europe, from Brazil, and even Australia." Shortill-Lopez explained that many of these service zealots work to earn enough money between each big sporting event so they can afford to take off and volunteer their time at the next major event. "They are true sports fanatics in every sense of the word," Shortill-Lopez commended with appreciation.

Dan Galbraith

Whomever they were, wherever they came from, and for whatever reason, Shortill-Lopez and her committee were beholden to the volunteer's incredible donation of time, energy and professionalism. "We could not have asked for more," she resolved, perhaps in reference to the volunteers' gift of themselves to the Games and their sheer numbers.

THE SALMON PEOPLE

Almost 24 hours a day for two-and-a-half weeks, they took tickets, chauffeured officials around the city, fed thousands of hungry athletes and quietly performed countless unseen acts of kindness to avert disaster and keep the Games rolling smoothly. They were the nearly 20,000 "salmon people" - volunteers who put their lives, families and jobs on hold to help out. For their hours of labour they received very little: a uniform of questionable fashion merit, a couple of hats and hopefully the satisfaction of knowing they were the backbone of a huge organizational machine that conceived, planned and made the Games a rousing success.

Almost immediately after Winnipeg bid for the Games, the call went out for volunteers. Organizers said they needed 18,000. Would that many willing Winnipeggers come forward? By the end of the Games, nearly 20,000 hearty souls had put their personal stamp on the XIIIth Pan American Games, showing visitors that "Friendly Manitoba" is more than just a slogan on the province's license plates. This should not have been a surprise. Winnipeg has a history of volunteerism that goes back to 1967, the first time the city hosted the Pan Am Games. More recently, volunteers came out in record numbers to help the city successfully host the World Junior Hockey Championships, the Brier Curling Tournament and the annual Fringe, Folk and Jazz Festivals, not to mention helping other Manitobans save their homes

Dan Galbraith

and businesses from the flood of the century in 1997. And then of course, there are the unsung thousands who help out charities, run community clubs and make sure little league games start on time.

Besides their assigned jobs - where they were, on occasion, accused of being slightly overzealous - Pan Am Games volunteers proved on a daily basis that Winnipeggers can't help but jump in when someone is in need. The province's reputation as the volunteer capital of Canada remains secure. "We couldn't have done it without them," thanked Bob McMahon, the Games' chief operating officer. "They made the decisions they were supposed to make and they made good decisions." Dick Schultz, general secretary of the United States Olympic Committee, had nothing but praise for them in his departing address in Winnipeg. "We can't say enough about the organization, the venues and especially the volunteers," he concluded. "They've been special."

SECOND GENERATION HOSPITALITY

Leonore Sanders had one of the most touching volunteer stories of the Pan Am Games. During the 1967 Games in Winnipeg, Sanders and her family billeted the Mexican women's diving team. "My daughter was a member of the Winnipeg swim team and our family decided to house some of the swimmers during the Games," informed Sanders. A long-lasting friendship was formed between the Sanders family and one of the Mexican divers, Norma Baraldi. After the '67 Games were long gone, letters and Christmas cards continued to be exchanged. "In 1973, when my daughter decided she wanted to go to Mexico and learn Spanish, I felt very comfortable with the idea knowing that Norma was there," confessed Sanders.

Years later the Sanders family went to visit Baraldi in Mexico over the Christmas holidays. After that, modern technology enabled the two families to keep in touch on a more regular basis. Both families bought a computer and started e-mailing each other to stay in touch. Then came the news that Norma's son would be competing at the '99 Pan Am Games. What better reason for a reunion. The Sanders family once again decided to billet athletes. They would be housing the Mexican men's water polo team including the team captain, Max Aguilar, Norma's 20-year-old son. "We were ecstatic to hear we would meet Norma's son and that she would be coming to Winnipeg to watch him compete," enthused Sanders.

Sanders informed her own family of the news and it all became extra special when her entire family said they would come to Winnipeg for a reunion. "It was the first time in nine years that our whole family was together in one spot," beamed Sanders. "I felt like I won gold at the Games."

WINNIPEG PROUD

BY RANDY TURNER, WINNIPEG FREE PRESS

I remember Neil Boisclair, a volunteer who collected the spit of the boxers, and wiped up the blood, sweat and tears of the less fortunate to enter the ring. "You take a shower sometimes," Boisclair said, and I winced. "But I have no problem with that. I put in for anything. As long as I'm here, doing my part it doesn't matter." Then Boisclair simply shrugged. Nothing special, just doing his part.

And around him, others in salmon-coloured shirts went about their business: checking gloves for tape, erecting and dismantling medal podiums, shepherding the hordes of athletes, fans and media to their proper places. Grunt work.

I remember when the 13th Pan Am Games began making some of us nervous. Ticket sales were stagnant and the only focus appeared to be on the fans and high-profile stars who weren't coming. The potential headlines were already printed: What if you held a Games and nobody showed up? There were fears it was going to be a natural dis-

VOLUNTEERS

SALGUEIRO • JASON SALOGNA • KYRA SAMPSON • MARC SAMSON • MONICA SAMUDA • JHOSA SANALANG • ALLISON SANDEMAN • KERNJEET SANDHU • SHARNJEET SANDHU • DIANE SANSOM • EMA SANTOS • EVELYN SANTOS • SYLVIA SANTOS • VIOLETTA SANTOS • SHERISSE SARAO • CAITLIN SARNA • GILLIAN SARNA • MEGHAN SARNA • ALISON SASS • STEVE SAUNDERS • TANYA SAUNDERS • BRIDGET SAVAGE • SHARON SAVICKEY • CYNTHIA SAWATSKY • LAUREN SAWICH • KEVIN SAWKA • TALIA SCATLIFF • LEEYA SCHACHTER • CARRIE SCHAEPE • AMY SCHAUB • PETER SCHILLING • KEVIN SCHITLER • SAMANTHA SCHMID • KARIN SCHMIDT • TEGAN SCHMIDT • GILLIAN SCHOFIELD • HAYLEY SCHOFIELD • SANDI SCHOLLENBERG • DANIEL SCHOLZ • ALAN SCHRODER • AUGUSTA SCHROEDER • KELLY SCHROEDER • RANI SCHROEDER • BRUCE SCHULZ • MATTHEW SCHULZ • MELISSA SCHULZ • C.T. SCHUMACK • CAROLYN SCHUREK • KRISTEN SCHUREK • GORD SCHURR • DAVID SCHWAKIN • ALEXANDRA SCHWEEN • QUINN KARLEY SCIBERRAS • BRITTANY SCOBIE • COURTNEE SCOBIE • CLARE SCOTT • KATHRYN SCOTT • KRISTY SCOTT • MEGAN KATHLEEN SCOTT • PETER SCOURAS • MEG SCRIMGER

"Working in accreditation, we were responsible for the first impression people had of the volunteer We took a lot of pride in starting them off happy, being good ambassadors for the city." *Walter Wa*

aster, like the flood. It seems such a long time ago. I wonder why I ever was doubtful.

It hit me, appropriately enough, beside a boxing ring. I was sitting beside CJOB broadcaster Bob Irving, who had just got off his cell phone. "There's 8,000 people at the beach volleyball final," he reported. "And they're going crazy." For the first time, I began to understand the legacy of the '67 Games - at least, for those of us who weren't around then - that you can't truly grasp from faded photographs or the memories of others. At the risk of sounding hackneyed, I felt an overwhelming sense of pride. In Manitobans.

Who are these people? And why is it, that when you really need them most, they're always there? My thoughts drifted back to The Flood of '97, and I began to see a correlation to that time, when our city was invaded by soldiers, not athletes, and every event was the sandbag toss. Instead of those salmon shirts, uniforms were hip-waders. I went home every night after another long day and watched Diana Swain tell me that everything was all right. And when it finally ended, when all the hard work was done, Burton Cummings sang.

We are a funny people sometimes. We live on a bald prairie that is frozen under ice and snow for six months of the year, yet many of us don't leave - a fact that surely must be puzzling to strangers. We too often feel that others are better, maybe because they didn't lose their hockey team or they build taller skyscrapers. But they are not.

In the end, I believe, you judge a community by those who make up its fabric, its history. You judge it by whether its residents, indeed, care about their city or each other. In many ways, we are a lot like a small town that refuses to fail, or look bad, especially if others are watching. We rally, that is what we do. Sometimes we win, sometimes we lose. But not because we don't care. That is why I felt that swell of pride that night; proud to be a Winnipegger. If that sounds hokey, so be it. The sentiment is real.

And years from now, another generation will be reminiscing about the way it was back in '99. "Remember those gawdawful pink shirts they made us wear?" they'll say. Me? I will not remember Steve Vezina, to be sure. I will remember Neil Boisclair, and those wearing shirts just like him, and the thousands upon thousands who came out to the Games in droves. Like a flood. How do I know this? Because I am a Manitoban, you see. And somewhere, in the distance, I can hear Burton Cummings singing.

Norm Lourenco

53

VOLUNTEERS

Dan Galbraith

DIGNITY & GRACE

Princess Anne's six-day visit to Manitoba was a triumph of tradition, good breeding and the extraordinary ability of one woman to present interest in countless briefly-met strangers in a manner that consistently appeared genuine and patient.

While there was none of the hysterical screaming, bouquet flinging and media scrums that used to greet Diana, Princess Anne's late sister-in-law, the dignified 49-year-old carried out the family business in Winnipeg with a firm handshake one subject at a time. For nearly a week - in smothering heat no less - the Queen's second-born maintained a wearying pace with a dawn-to-dusk touring schedule. Dressed simply, usually in a dress and her ubiquitous gloves, she makes something very difficult look quite natural. With grace and dignity, she effortlessly put those who met her at ease.

The princess repeatedly applauded Manitobans for their prowess in hosting the Pan Am Games. "I hope all of you in Manitoba feel a real sense of achievement for bringing the Games here," she commended at a departing ceremony at Lower Fort Garry's Big House. "I assure you, the athletes I have met are delighted to be here."

VOLUNTEERS

SUMMER CLEANING

Ask anyone in Winnipeg. The city may never have looked so good as it did for the 1999 Pan Am Games, the biggest event in its history. It was not only governments that swept up the dustballs, hoisted flags and welcome banners, and decorated with new plants and flowers. Business people and homeowners also did their part to ensure that the city looked its best for the projected 100,000 visitors who arrived in Winnipeg for the Games.

The Exchange District Business Improvement Zone reported that a great number of businesses in the area called for suggestions on what they could do for the Games. While the Exchange BIZ was already decking out the area with pleasing flora, many local businesses across the city chose to showcase their shops with extra flowers and Pan Am banners. Garth Steek, city councilor for River Heights, commented on the many homeowners who used the Games as a source of motivation for home fix-ups and a mid-summer's renewed interest in lawn care. "There's no question there was a great deal of pride surrounding the Games," he observed.

In addition to a good sweeping of major streets and Pan Am routes, and a stepped up litter-control program, city hall underwent a dramatic makeover to become Winnipeg House for the Games. Stylish floral arrangements, colourful benches and an outdoor stage were added to the seat of civic government. The council building also received some attention, being transformed into an art gallery with works from local and international artists.

Total bill for the make-over? Public works cautioned Winnipeggers not to be fooled by popular wisdom suggesting that the city spent millions of dollars fixing roads and other infrastructure for the Games. Only $100,000 in additional money was spent to help clean up the community, a city spokesperson revealed.

AIR WATCH

It is quite possible that one of the most enduring images of the Games for Winnipeggers will be something that was not found on any of the fields of play, but high above them. The Goodyear blimp, the world's largest airship, created a seventeen-day buzz on the ground as the subject of interest and intrigue for many.

Sporting a Canadian flag off its tail, the massive Spirit of Akron, the 12-year-old biggest brother of Goodyear's fleet of seven airships worldwide earned its keep in Winnipeg as the world's most recognizable corporate billboard. It's also considered to be the best place to mount a camera for what television people call the "beauty shot." With a cruising speed of 56 kilometres per hour and lifted by the simplest of the inert gases in the periodic table, the helium-filled blimp drifted above the Pan Am venues each day providing images as part of CBC-TV's coverage.

For those who found themselves within earshot of the 63-metre-long airship, most were surprised how much noise it made. With a maximum weight of 6,800 kilograms, the Spirit of Akron relies on the roar of a pair of 420-horsepower engines flanking the eight-seat passenger compartment with its open cockpit as its power source.

The blimp has a top speed of 104 km/h and houses a fuel tank that holds 1,612 litres of jet fuel, allowing for a maximum of 12 hours in the air. Operationally, as the blimp rises, the helium in the envelope expands, increasing the internal pressure. Two air bags, one housed in the nose and one in the tail, are deflated through external valves to compensate. The higher the blimp rises, the more air that must be released from the air bags.

Dan Galbraith

PAN A'MANIACS by Lindor Reynolds

They were rabidly dedicated supporters of the Pan Am Games. They were equipped

VOLUNTEERS

with their official Pan Am playing cards, sweatshirts, coffee mugs, collector's spoons, baseball caps and pennants. Their homes are filled with Pato keychains, stuffed dolls, T-shirts and a fanatic favourite - suction cup Pato to stick to their car's rear window. But that's not all. They frequented The Forks every night, had tickets to every bowling game and water skiing event, were on a first-name basis with the Brazilian track team and knew the first 45 seconds to all 42 national anthems. They were Pan A'maniacs and time is the only cure.

Heather Van Der Lek, an esthetician at Jerry's Hair Design, was painting the Pan Am logo on people's thumb nails and big toes. For five dollars a pair, she used nail polish, a fine paintbrush and "a really steady hand" to create her art. "It's bright, it's colourful and it's a lot of fun," she commented. "The Canadian flag on finger and toenails was a popular choice."

Maybe something a little more permanent for the hard-core Pan A'maniac? Maybe a commemorative tatoo? "We can't actually do the Pan Am logo because of the corporate tie -in," explained a friendly gent at Tattoos By Strider. "We do Maple Leafs. For $80 or $90 you can get a really nice one." If body art was a little too alternative, the fun-loving Pan

Dan Galbraith

A'maniac may have been spotted sipping specialty Pan Am spirits at a club around town. Maybe a Breast Stroke, a combination of McGuiness Blue Curacao and Creme de Banane. Maybe a Shot Put - Kahlua, Irish Cream and more Creme de Banane. The Equestrian fans lapped up the Sauza Steeplechase, a simple mix of tequila and lime. How are these different from any other shooter? Not important to a true Pan A'maniac.

Pan Am sushi roll? At Wasabi Sushi Bar, they were serving up a smoked goldeye, cucumber, sliced onion, Japanese radish sprout roll all wrapped up in smoked salmon. It was a wacky kind of Pan Am treat but owner Cho Venevongsa ("Sushi Joe") maintained he had a hit on his hands.

What an experience for even the most ardent Pan A'maniac. Fed and watered with Pan Am grub and spirits. Nails look great. The tattoo is healing. What's left? Maybe a bouquet of flowers. A stop at Academy Florists on Marion, where the windows were decorated in Pan Am colours and a sign welcomed visitors. This would be the place to buy a Pan Am bouquet, right? Wrong. No defilement at this flower shop. Forsaking any entrepreneurial spirit, shop

VOLUNTEERS

Dan Galbraith

owner Reza Mohammadzadh avowed, "We are happy the Games are here, but we shouldn't mix it with money. We just want to let everyone know we are happy they are here." And that right there just may be the ultimate in Pan A'mania.

AMBASSADORS OF FUN

They were colourful characters and they competed every day - competed for attention that is. Their marathon of meeting and greeting - and clowning around - actually began long before the Games' opening night, but once the XIIIth Pan American Games were officially underway, it was an all-out sprint, an endless stream of activity and energy wrapped up in seven-foot suits. Taking time to interact with kids and adults, athletes and spectators, it was the duty of Pato and Lorita, the mascots, to ensure that the fun and energy of the Games never lapsed.

The job entailed 9,000 hugs and at least as many cozy photo poses every day. The mascots were hot - really hot - in popularity and body temperature as some days mercury levels mercilessly topped 34 degrees Celsius on the outside of their suits. The mascot team of 30 feathered friends - 19 for Games-time - shared eight suits among them, four for each character. A ton of planning, coordination and dedication by the animated crew brought Lorita Panamericana the Pan American Parrot and Pato Panamericano the Pan American Wood Duck to life.

Designed by International Mascot Corporation in Alberta, the winning wood duck was chosen from among 18 submissions considered for Pan Am mascotship. Children at Winnipeg's Voyageur Elementary School came up with the mascot's name. Pato Panamericano is Spanish for "Pan American duck." The name was chosen from some 100 entries submitted by Manitoba schools in the Pan Am's "Name-the-Mascot" contest.

The mascots represented the sportsmanship and camaraderie of the Games. They communicate in a universal language of gestures, movement and touch. To some, it would seem an enviable job, with many fringe benefits. Everybody loves a mascot, kids and adults alike; admittance to events is free and goofiness is what is expected and reinforced by crowd and athlete support. "We got to see the best of the Games," explained Lorita. "Personally, I think we had the best job of all the volunteers." Mascot Coordinator Collen Deckert had nothing but praise for her committed flock. "They did it with heart and soul."

VILLAGE STARS

She has the warm smiling face that visiting athletes came to love ... and pinch. "They called me 'omere' or 'oma' or whatever Spanish people call their grandmas," 75-year-old Reta Barrie said with a smile. "And I guess pinching cheeks is a show of affection in South America. My cheeks were so sore, but it felt good too."

Barrie was part of the "early-morning crew" of volunteers at the University of Manitoba athlete village dining hall.

VOLUNTEERS

Dan Galbraith

At 4:45 a.m. every day of the Games, the Winnipeg grandmother of two climbed out of bed to be at the university in time for her six a.m. shift. Her duties included greeting and guiding athletes through breakfast.

If laughter is the best medicine, then Barrie, who had her hip replaced only months before the Games and sported a purple shade around her eye from a cataract operation just days before her duties began, has many more good times ahead. Barrie started her volunteer stint on crutches, courtesy of her hip operation, but was getting around with the aid of a cane and her self-decorated Pan Am Games running shoes before her tour of duty was complete. She said her biggest reward was meeting people like Rita Wagner, another star volunteer at the dining hall.

Wagner, a 50-year-old "proud Canadian" who immigrated to Manitoba from Germany 18 years ago, raved about her own volunteer experience. "I helped a Mexican coach," recalled the mother of two, "and he gave me an angel pendant. He thought I was an angel for helping him." Wagner, among other volunteer staff, were able to convince the kitchen to offer hot milk, a breakfast staple in South America, and tabasco, a favorite egg garnish of Mexican athletes.

Doug Chandler, volunteer head of food services, said workers like Barrie and Wagner made everyone's experience better. "It was a wonderful place in the morning for athletes," he contended. "The volunteer spirit was infectious. They were the superstars of this event."

What's next for the two superstars? "I have got to get myself to Australia," declared Barrie, referring to the 2000 Olympics in Sydney. "Or the 2003 Pan Ams in the Dominican Republic," chimed in Wagner.

THE LITTLEST HELPER

Eight-year-old Lauren Schinkel was the youngest volunteer to give of her time at the Pan Am Games. Volunteer rules for the Games stated that helpers had to be at least 16 years old to participate. However, there are always exceptions to the rule. If allowing younger volunteers to participate in certain sports would help promote that sport then it was permitted. "My mom came home and said she was going to volunteer at handball," told Lauren. "I wanted to help too."

Lauren's mother has competed in handball for 20 years and Lauren hopes one day she'll be able to compete too.

VOLUNTEERS

CIA WILSON • JOANNE WILSON • BROOKE WILTON • JOY WILTON • DANIELLE WINCH • HEATHER WINDATT • KELLI WINDSOR- BROWN • AMELIA WIRCH • VANESSA WIRTH • STEPHANIE WISHART • JENNIFER WITTEVRONGEL • LAURA WITTIG • RUTH WIWCHAR • JEREMY WIWCHARYK • GERALD WOJCIECHOWSKI • CECILIA WOJCIK • ANTHONY WOJTAS • JESSICA WOLF • GORDON WOLFE • ANDREA KATHLEEN WOLFRAM • MARY WOLKE • EDMOND WONG • KEN WONG • LILLIAN WONG • QUINCY WONG • SHANNON WONG • MEAGAN WOO • BRITTANY WOOD • CRYSTAL WOOD • DELANEY WOOD • JANELLE WOOKEY • JEREMIE WOOKEY • NICOLE WORKS • WINNIE WORONIUK • DELLA WORONOWSKI • VAL WOSTAS • AMANDA WOWRYK • PHILIP WOZNEY • PATRICK WRIGHT • SIMONE WRIGHT • TRACY WRIGHT • AMY WU • KRISTOPHER WYLIE • DANIELLE YAKIWCHUK • MICHELLE YALLITS • MARY YANKE • MAUREEN YANUSZEWSKI • YVONNE YEATS • VAL YERENIUK • ERICK YIP • SHEILA YOSYK • TIM YUEN • SLANA YURASCHUK • STEPHEN YURKIW • JULIE ZABUDNY • BARRY ZACHARIAS • BETHANY ZACHARIAS • MARGARET ZADWORNEY • KELLY- ANNE ALEXANDRA ZAHY-

"I've spent most of my life as a professional volunteer but nothing has ever approached the magnitude these Games. The Games have broadened my horizons." *Wendy Waggoner, Co-Chair of Spectator Servic*

"I'd like to be one of the athletes in these Games." But this time around the enthusiastic youngster was in charge of running after missed balls during the handball matches. Volunteers at the Games had to follow strict rules, which for an eight-year-old could sometimes be challenging. "We can't lie down in our chairs, like slouch," she announced. "We're not allowed electric things (like radios) except for watches." And then her least favourite of all the rules: "When the ref moves around the court, we have to follow and wipe up all the sweat off the floor." Even after explaining that rule to her fourth grade friends, she said that they still considered her lucky. "They tell me they wish they could be me because I get to see the athletes up close and I'm right there on the court with them." Lauren was inspired by the spirit of the Games. You never know, one day she might be front and center as a competitor. But for now, she sure has a lot to talk about at school.

Norm Lourenco

YOUNG AT HEART NEED ONLY APPLY

At eighty-seven years old, Violet Weir was the senior stateswoman at the Pan Am Games, and with the energy of volunteers fifty years her junior no less. Weir volunteered at the 1967 Games and couldn't resist throwing her name into the hat in 1999 as well. "I love sports; I'd love to still be playing them. I have made some wonderful friends through sports and I didn't want to miss out on that opportunity at the 1999 Pan Ams."

Weir is no stranger to answering the call for volunteer time. She has been involved in local charities since she came to Winnipeg in 1946. "It allows me to be a part of the community and I never miss out on any gossip that way either." In her younger days, Weir participated in a plethora of sports. "I competed in curling, skating, badminton, speed skating and I even played a little hockey," she chuckled. "But I also love crafts."

In 1967 Weir worked a full-time job by day and volunteered at the Pan Am Pool at night. "I didn't get to see any other events; there wasn't any time." Now that she is retired, Weir had a list of events she wanted to see. "I love to watch equestrian events and I hear there is inline skating ... that would be quite enjoyable," she voiced. "And since I competed in softball and baseball when I was younger, I'd love to catch those events too." Although she did not get to attend the Opening Ceremony, she was glued to her television set for the entire show. "They call us 'Friendly Manitoba' and I sure felt that way when I was watching." The giving nature of Manitobans proved to be contagious. One of Weir's new-found friends, an out-of-towner from Ontario, hand delivered a free ticket to the Closing Ceremony to Weir just hours before the Pan Am send-off party. Violet Weir, the Games most senior volunteer, was on her feet most of the evening waving good-bye to a sea of new friends.

Norm Lourenco

VOLUNTEERS

A PASSION FOR PINS

They call themselves "Pinheads" and take it as a compliment when others call them the same. They are passionate pin traders - lapel-type pins - and their hobby has become so popular it could be classified unofficially as the 42nd sport at the Pan Am Games. They come from all over the world in search of the most unique and most popular pins.

The sports-scene pin collecting craze originated at the 1980 Winter Olympics in Lake Placid, where spectators covered their hats with pins attracting media attention and new-found traders. In 1984, at the Summer Olympics in Los

Angeles, the media labeled all those with pin-covered hats as "Pinheads".

Winnipeg's Games organizers anticipated that come Games-time, the city would be crawling with "Pinheads" and others just interested in how it all works. To meet the projected demand, Manitoba Telecom Services Inc. (MTS) was quick to climb aboard the pin-trading phenomenon. Accordingly, the majority of Pan Am pin-trading took place at the MTS Pin-Trading Centre located at The Forks, the heart of the Pan Am Games entertainment district. But why did Manitoba's telephone company get involved in pin-trading? "I think it likely stems from our general commitment to community," offered Therese Mickelson, Public Affairs Co-ordinator for MTS. "MTS does a lot of sponsorships and we do a lot of things to help events like the Pan Am Games be a success. We were the first sponsor to sign on when it was announced that Winnipeg would be the host city and MTS immediately looked at ways in which it could participate," Mickelson added. "We had great success with sponsoring the pin-trading tent at the Canada Games and felt it would be something we'd like to get involved with again." Mickelson admitted that when it comes to pin-trading there may not be a strong telecommunications link but it is MTS's way of giving back. "Pin-trading has become tremendously popular and you meet some really interesting people; we thought this would be a great way to participate."

No matter what time of day or night, the area in and around the Pin-Trading Centre was always busy. The doors to the Centre may have been locked after closing time, but that didn't stop the die-hard pin-traders from sticking around to do what they do best. "This is a fabulous way for me to spend my time now that I'm retired," explained one Pinhead. "I meet a lot of people, I travel around the world and get to be involved with all the biggest sporting events. What more could I want?" He chuckled, " I just wish my wife agreed with me."

Norm Lourenco

VOLUNTEERS

Mickelson confessed that before she understood the ins and outs of pin-trading she wondered what all the fuss was about. But now she appreciates the art of pin-trading and has a new respect for those who dedicate time to it. "It is an inexpensive way to remember an event. For six dollars or so, you can get a unique souvenir," relished Mickelson. "I've noticed that athletes and pin-traders who don't speak a lick of English can always spark up a conversation over the word 'pin'. Pin-trading seems to have its own language ... it breaks down barriers, it's a way to meet and get to know some-one - it's actually quite fascinating to watch."

More than 200 pins were designed for the Games, featuring events, countries and sponsors. The hot items turned out to be the "Pins of the Day". MTS released 2,000 'day specific' collector pins each morning. Pinheads were regularly lined up around the block before the Centre's doors opened to ensure they got the "Pin of the Day".

In the spirit of promoting Canada and Canadian-made products throughout the Pan Am Games, Canadian Pin Manufacturer Laurie Artiss Ltd. was chosen to supply the pins for the event. This Saskatchewan company is no stranger to big sporting events or the pin-trading frenzy. It has created and supplied pins for the 1997 Canada Summer Games and the Canadian Olympic Association.

Mickelson said that one memory that she will carry with her long after the Games is how passionate the Pinheads are about their hobby. "You've got to respect their passion. And I must admit, I've got a few pins that may be hot on the trading block next Games." What is certain however, is that each one of these hobbyists is already qualified and pre-pared for their spot at the next big Games. See you in Sydney, Pinheads.

MOSQUITO LAND

The 1999 Pan Am Games earned Winnipeg the reputation of being the most organized in Pan Am history. And deservedly so. The city didn't miss a beat, not with transportation, not with venues, and not even in dealing with their pesky little mosquitoes.

The Winnipeg Free Press, in its daily *Pan Am Games Special* section, provided readers - particularly those visit-ing from around the world - with valuable insect information and a little chuckle each morning. The City of Winnipeg submitted a daily blurb about the mosquito count in and around the city. Athletes, fans and others asso-ciated with the Games were warned - do not venture out into Mosquito Land unprepared.

Visitors to the city couldn't help but wonder how the city conducted a daily mosquito count and friendly Manitoba was ready to explain. Randy Gadawski, a Winnipeg entomologist, happily provided the information. "Did you know only female mosquitoes bite and they need sugar to survive and reproduce? That's why humans are their favourite meal; our blood is a convenient source of sugar." Gadawski had more. "Winnipeg is home to 38 out of 2,500 species of mosquitoes worldwide, which is half the number found in Canada."

VOLUNTEERS

Each summer the city gauges the severity of the mosquito onslaught by setting 13 traps throughout Winnipeg. In an average year, Gadawski finds 100 female mosquitoes per trap each day. Any more than that, and it's time to take extra precautions for an evening outside. The City of Winnipeg spends $1.2 million annually in mosquito control, spent largely on conducting spraying programs. But Gadawski asks residents and visitors to spare the little pests whenever possible. They do serve a useful purpose, he promoted. Mosquitoes help pollinate certain types of flowers, including Manitoba's sunflowers.

WHO'S GOT TICKETS?

Skepticism circled harshly before the official opening of the Games. Would Winnipeggers be there, would they come out as spectators? Organizers' fear of empty seats was exacerbated by the fact that Winnipeg, in the past fifteen months, had hosted the Briar Curling Tournament, the Grey Cup and the World Junior Hockey Championships. Along with the numerous other local events and festivals that occur every year in Winnipeg and surrounding areas, the distinct possibility of a poor turnout had naysayers predicting the worst. But true to their reputation, the city turned up at the last minute and tickets began to go quickly. From the headlines that had screamed "No Show" the media were soon reporting on "unexpected, but welcome sellouts."

To hit the break-even mark, organizers had hoped to sell 500,000 tickets for the Games. The total ticket sales revenue of nearly $12 million was about $1 million shy of the projected budget. But, a collective sigh of relief from organizers could almost be heard over the near-sellout crowd's welcome of the Guess Who at the Closing Ceremony.

Kim Browning, Vice President of Ticket Sales for Winnipeg's Pan Am Games Society (PAGS), knew Winnipeggers supported the idea of the city hosting the Games. The general consensus was that it would be a good thing for the city; and everyone seemed proud that it was happening. Studies showed that ninety-nine per cent of Winnipeggers knew the Games were coming to Winnipeg. "I'm not sure who the other one per cent was, but ninety-two per cent thought it would be good for the city. That's a very high margin," commented Browning. "Winnipeg is known as a 'walk-up town.' We knew that those who were extreme keeners, the sports nuts, were going to buy early and they did." What organizers didn't anticipate, at least not for certain, was the suspense that they would have to endure before ticket revenues were realized.

"Our market research for these Games at about ten months out asked people how much they were going to spend, what sports they really wanted to see, were they going to attend the Opening Ceremony and when were they planning on doing their buying," explained Browning. "They told us they were coming." Browning and company programmed

GIVE HER A MEDAL

They called her "Media Mom" up at Birds Hill Park, and if medals were being handed out by journalists at the Pan Am Games, 42-year-old Joan Wiebe is one volunteer who might have trotted up to the podium. Wiebe picked up the endearing nickname for her dedication not only to the people competing in the equestrian events at the Games, but to the crew telling the world about them as well.

Wiebe single-handedly fed a herd of international journalists covering the Games' equestrian events. Every day, she dished out home-made sandwiches - egg salad, turkey and ham - to at least 15 media types working at that venue. "I did it because basically there was nothing there for them. And they needed something quick, fast and on the run," Wiebe observed. Journalists chipped in five dollars a day for groceries.

"This is something we'll never get to do again, a time when there are so man different nations in our country where we are able to assist." *Doug Delmarqu*

Dan Galbraith

their marketing around that premise. "We did a bit of advertising last summer [1998], but we didn't really spend our advertising money until about March or April of '99. They told us they were going to buy late, and they did. I had a lot of sleepless nights this spring."

But Winnipeggers were not lying. Browning saw incredible surges in ticket sales in the last two months preceding the Games. Then, in the last two weeks leading up to Games-time, ticket sales sky-rocketed. The torrid pace continued throughout the seventeen days of competition hitting anywhere from eight to fifteen thousand tickets per day. The traditional events were popular, but the interest in the non-traditional spectator events surprised everyone, including Browning. "I think that if we asked ourselves two years ago if baseball was going to be this popular we would have said 'no,'" Browning confessed. Mixing in the excitement of the Canada versus U.S. extra-inning game and the reputation of the Cuban team all helped to raise people's awareness that the caliber of the tournament was extremely high. Throw in a brand-new ballpark that people had fallen in love with and the fact that it was an Olympic qualifier and the perfect scenario was set for that venue. It was believed that the excitement that baseball generated spilled over into the lesser spectator-popular sports as well.

The gold-medal soccer match was sold out before the competitors were qualified to compete. Softball, particular-

VOLUNTEERS

ly women's, was popular, as were the track and field finals. Sometimes it is pure sport appreciation, sometimes a little nostalgia for times past and sometimes it is pure star power that gets fans anticipating the competition. Interestingly, some of the less-popular sports received enormous support from the community. Water Polo had a great draw, partially due to the men's endearment to the fans during the Opening Ceremony. The women's team also had generous crowds, despite being a first-time event at the Games. Roller hockey was an expected crowd-pleaser. There were even scalpers out at select events, including gymnastics. Under-exposed sports like Team Handball and Field Hockey were thrilled by the crowd turnout to their events, not only for the support of the athletes competing, but for the exposure to the sport itself.

As part of the Games' overall strategy, an incentive was provided for the "keeners" - those who purchased tickets to the Games early. For them, souvenir tickets were issued. "Specially designed as a commemorative souvenir," Browning described, "they had a very small ticket stub tear, so not much of the ticket was lost when used. Their intention was to thank those who committed to tickets early in the game."

Sales were nurtured by low-scale ticket prices. Tickets ranged from $8 to $40. "The Society had always been focused on making the Games accessible to all segments of the community," exhorted Don MacKenzie, President of the Pan Am Games Society. "This was reflected in the ticket prices."

Another program embraced by Games organizers, as well as the corporate community, was the "Share the Games Community Ticket Program." The initiative accommodated corporations who had approached the committee wishing to contribute something to the Games by providing an opportunity to purchase tickets for community members who might not have had the means to attend the Games otherwise. This goodwill drive wasn't restricted to corporations only. A number of individuals donated tickets as well. "I can remember a call from a very sweet older woman," Browning recalled. "She knew she wasn't going to get out to any of the events. She wrote us a cheque for $200 which we turned into multiple tickets and forwarded to The United Way." The United Way wasn't the only charity involved in the program, but it provided significant support through ticket distribution. PAGS also turned a number of sponsored and donated tickets over to other social agencies for distribution, including Winnipeg Harvest, The Manitoba Metis Federation and the Assembly of Manitoba Chiefs.

The United Way also set up a ticket exchange program. "If an individual had tickets, and for whatever reason couldn't attend the event, then there was the opportunity to drop those tickets off and allow The United Way to do their best, through their membership association, to get them out to somebody who could use them," Browning detailed.

Browning noted that the most enjoyable part of his Games experience was getting out to events and watching families interact with each other and the crowd. "The amount of children at all the events really impressed me. People definitely made this a family experience ... moms and dads out with the kids. Peanuts, popcorn, hot dogs ... the whole pack-

"For Winnipeg as a city I think there will be a great legacy from the Games. Walking through the city now, there's a lot of pride. Everything just seemed to come together." *Duncan Dejardi*

age was fun to watch." Browning's own family was equally caught up in it all. "My whole family dyed their hair the different colours of the Pan Am logo. We've got green, blue, red and goldish blonde," he smiled.

LIKE KIDS IN A CANDY STORE

Marnie McBean slipped the red shorts on under her pale blue mini-dress. "Too big," proclaimed the Canadian rowing champion, hurrying to slide them off and put them in the "out" pile. Behind a screen in a lounge at the University of Manitoba's athlete village was where the Canadian team got rigged up in its official gear - a process called "staging."

McBean sat down as the Canadian Olympic Association's Michelle Comeau went through the list and handed her each item from a red duffel bag. Roots has been the official supplier to the Canadian Olympic Association since 1988 and has the contract until 2004 (the Roots 'poor-boy' hat took the world by storm at Nagano). When the Games are over, the athletes either keep the clothes, or trade them off with athletes from other countries.

First, McBean was issued the podium wear, which doubles for parades. This was the outfit athletes wore when receiving a medal. It was also what they were wearing when they raced around Winnipeg Stadium on opening night: white track jacket with a red maple leaf on the back, red tearaway pants, a short-sleeved V-necked shirt, sport sandals and a red ball cap. Some of it too big, some too small. McBean requested a size 43 sandal instead of the 40. "You get caught up wearing team wear; it's a way of identifying each other," said McBean, adding that at every competition one item becomes especially popular. At the Pan Am Games, she thought it might be the podium V-necked shirt.

On to the events wear, for special functions such as the team reception. Comeau pulled out a white golf shirt, chino pants and black belt. The pants fit perfectly as did the size 30 belt. McBean needed a larger golf shirt, for a more roomy fit. Her off-water look is quite a bit different from when she's competing. "My rowing T-shirts are very small and the shorts are tight. You don't want to get them caught in the oars or slides," she explained, noting that athletes bring their own competitive gear.

For casual wear, McBean was given a sweatshirt, red and grey T-shirts, red shorts, black shorts and socks. Also in the bag was a back-pack, fanny-pack and a bag of trading pins. The bags were provided by Samboro Luggage. Carla Anderson was the staging manager; she's the one who transformed University College's kitchen into an Olympic-sized clothing warehouse. What was the athletes' response to their goodie bags? "It's like a candy store," laughed McBean.

YOU'RE SPEAKING MY LANGUAGE

Winnipeg's eleven-year-old Cristina Meadows became part of a new family during the Games: all the Cuban athletes staying at the Pan Am Village near Portage la Prairie, Cristina's home town. Along with her sisters - Nancy, 19, and Cynthia, 14 - and their parents John and Maria, Cristina provided translating services for the Spanish-speaking athletes at the village. But it was the Cubans who took a real shine to the girls, hauling them on shopping trips and letting them sit on the bench with them during games and practices. It all started when Nancy decided she wanted to be a volunteer at the village.

When the organizers discovered everyone in the family spoke Spanish, they wanted the whole family. John was born in Canada but moved to Mexico as a child. He returned to Canada with his own family 14 years ago, just after Cynthia was born. They all speak Spanish at home so they can communicate with their family back home in Mexico, told John.

As the girls prepared to run off to join the team for its practice, Maria cast a wistful eye at the chattering Cubans. "The family is going to miss them when they finish their games and head home," she revealed. "Some have already asked us if we'd like to go and live with them in Cuba," smiled Cynthia sensing the irony.

VOLUNTEERS

Special thanks to **Panasonic.** for the support of this section.

The Pan American Games are the second largest multi-sport event in the world after the Summer Olympic Games. Winnipeg's 1999 Pan Ams were the third-largest athletic competition ever held in North America, behind only by the Olympics in Los Angeles in 1984 and Atlanta in '96.

THE COMPETITION

PAN AMERICAN SPORTS ORGANIZATION

The Pan American Sports Organization (PASO) is comprised of 42 member nations representing North, South, and Central America and the Caribbean. There are three countries from North America, twelve from South America, seven from Central America, and twenty from the Caribbean. PASO consists of an elected Executive Committee, including the president, Mario Vazquez Rana from Mexico City. Rana also presides over Mexico's Olympic Committee, the Association of National Olympic Committees (ANOC) and is an International Olympic Committee (IOC) member.

Dan Galbraith

Each of the Pan American countries has a National Olympic Committee (NOC) that belongs to PASO, one of five Continental Sports Organizations that fall under the auspices of the IOC. The IOC is the sole body responsible for the Olympic Games and the NOCs deal directly with the IOC where their Olympic participation is concerned. The Pan American Games are held every four years during the summer preceding the Olympic Games, and follow a format similar to the Olympics. The sports program of the Pan American Games is larger than the Olympic line-up, celebrating a number of sports that are not in the Olympic program but popular in Pan American countries. Approximately 80 per cent of the sports on the Pan Am program are Olympic sports.

68

Don Gaudette

Dan Galbraith

IN THE FIELD

The official languages of PASO are Spanish and English. Its emblem contains a torch superimposed over five concentric circles. At least one of the colours of the circles (yellow, green, white, red and blue) appears on every national flag in the Americas. PASO's motto - "America, Espirito, Sport, Fraternite" - incorporates four of the languages common to the Americas - Spanish, Portuguese, English and French.

SOCCER

ORIGINS Some form of soccer was played by several ancient civilizations and was being played around the world by the Middle Ages. "The famous game of ball" on a Shrove Tuesday in 1175 in London, England, is still a tradition in some parts of England. The game evolved to the modern-day version in Britain's public schools and, in 1863 in London, the Football Association was formed and the initial set of laws was drawn up. The Federation Internationale de Football Association (FIFA), formed in 1904, is best known for the World Cup, which is held every four years. Soccer was first played at the

69

Keith Levit

PLENTY OF PROMISE AND PAIN AFTER KICKING OFF THE PAN AM GAMES WOMEN'S SOCCER TOURNAMENT WITH A TRIO OF TRIUMPHS AND PLENTY OF PROMISE, THREE STRAIGHT LOSSES TO FINISH THE COMPETITION LEFT THE WOMEN'S TEAM EMPTY, BOTH EMOTIONALLY AND IN THE HARDWARE DEPARTMENT. TWICE, IN AS MANY GAMES, THEIR MEDAL HOPES WERE DASHED BY LOSSES ON PENALTY KICK SHOOTOUTS - FIRST TO MEXICO IN THE SEMI-FINAL MATCH AND THEN TO COSTA RICA IN THE BRONZE MEDAL GAME.

VOLUNTEERS

Dan Galbraith

Olympics in the 1900 Paris Games. While Canadians call this game soccer, it is called football in most countries and at the Olympics.

MEXICO STRIKES AGAIN

Winnipeg has proven to be magical for Mexico's men's soccer squads. They've won gold twice in the sport in Pan Am competition; both were won in Winnipeg - 1967 and 1999. The heavily favoured Mexicans topped their scrappy opponents from Honduras with a 3-1 win in the gold-medal final at a packed Winnipeg Soccer Complex. Yet, while marvelous Mexico got the medal it expected, the silver medal winners were seemingly just as pleased with their own outcome. It was the first soccer medal for Honduras in the 48-year history of the Games.

To the disappointment of a rain-soaked and wind-bitten sellout crowd of about 8,000, there was no patriotic party for the Canadians after the bronze medal game. The Canadian men's soccer team had shown a great deal of progress in the tournament, but succumbed to the U.S. team in a very physical match that was not as close as the 2-1 final score suggested.

VOLUNTEERS

EMERGING STAR

Before arriving in Winnipeg, Sarah Barradas only ever signed her name on term papers and the occasional bank slip. But after receiving requests for her autograph at every Pan Am turn, she admitted she was a little confounded by all the attention that came her way. "It's just way too weird," exclaimed the 16-year-old Canadian soccer phenomenom.

Barradas, from Richmond Hill, Ont., emerged as Canada's most dangerous weapon and future mainstay on the pitch. But "star" of the 20-and-under squad is something of which the sensational striker has yet to become comfortable. "I'm not looking for the spotlight," Barradas confessed. "We all have roles on this team ... mine is to score goals," she countered. "I just want to play well for my country."

Barradas strapped on her first set of shin-guards for her first kicks at the ball when she was just four years old. She explained that she never thought the game of soccer would take her anywhere. She simply dreamed of being a lawyer like her father, or maybe a doctor or a vet. Gone are those childhood aspirations. The natural progression, as she now sees it, means finishing high school, securing a scholarship to a top U.S. school, and cracking the Canadian team in time for the next World Cup. Together with that may just come a few more autograph requests.

Norm Lourenco

Dan Galbraith

BASEBALL & SOFTBALL

O R I G I N S The game that English settlers in North America called "stoolball" went through a lot of changes on its way to becoming America's national pastime. The first "officially" recognized game is said to have taken place in Hoboken, New Jersey in 1846, using rules that resemble today's softball more than today's baseball. Baseball was a demonstration sport at the Olympics eight times prior to becoming an official sport in Barcelona in 1992. Only women compete in softball at the Olympic level.

"THIS IS THE MOST FUN I'VE EVER HAD IN MY LIFE. TO SEE THE JOY ON THESE PLAYERS' FACES MAKES ME VERY PROUD OF THEM. WE FINISHED WITH THE BEST RECORD IN THE TOURNAMENT AND WON CANADA'S FIRST-EVER PAN AM MEDAL IN BASEBALL."
ERNIE WHITT, MANAGER, CANADIAN MEN'S BASEBALL TEAM

BASEBALL HISTORY

The Winnipeg Games marked the first time in history that professional baseball players competed in the Pan American Games. Mario Vazquez Rana, president of the Pan

VOLUNTEERS

American Sports Organization (PASO), admitted that the inclusion of pro athletes in the Games has not been a smooth transition. "We are going through a time where combining professional and amateur athletes is one of the major problems that PASO is dealing with," Rana revealed, noting that some of the smaller countries are frustrated because they cannot compete with larger teams stacked with professional players. "But we have to do what is done in the Olympic Games - we can not go backwards," Rana contends.

JUST SIGN HERE

As the story went, sports agents lurked along the edges of the Canadian Forces Base athlete village trying to snag the best Cuban baseball players with promise of big bucks. Cuban officials reported that the suspected

In Havana, Fidel Castro welcomed his champion baseball team home with an attempt to mend his fraying ties with Canada by praising Foreign Affairs Minister Lloyd Axworthy for congratulating the Cuban ball players.

Norm Lourenco

VOLUNTEERS

Dan Galbraith

scouts were offering up contracts worth millions of dollars in an effort to steal their elite athletes. Jose Ramon Fernandez Alvarez, president of the Cuban Olympic Committee and vice-president of the country's committee of ministers, contended that besides the economic factors, a morbid issue was at hand: "these people with money are trying to drain our muscles and brains." He pledged that Cuban athletes had handed over written offers received through the fence ranging between $5 million and $10 million. Supt. Don McLean, a City of Winnipeg police officer with Pan Am security, confirmed that security personnel had witnessed people making attempts to contact Cuban athletes. It was no secret that major league scouts waited to get a look at the Cuban talent at the baseball venue. Without a doubt, there were some players worth watching on the Cuban team.

75

FIDEL CASTRO SPOKE OUT FORCEFULLY DURING THE GAMES,
LASHING OUT AT CANADA IN HIS ANNUAL REVOLUTION DAY SPEECH.
"WE HAVE NEVER SEEN SO MANY TRICKS, SO MUCH FILTH IN THE PAN
AMERICAN GAMES," ESPOUSED CASTRO. THE CUBAN LEADER WAS
ANGRY THAT PROFESSIONALS WERE ALLOWED INTO THE BASEBALL
EVENT AND THAT CUBAN DEFECTIONS IN WINNIPEG WERE BEING
PLAYED UP AND ENCOURAGED. FOREIGN AFFAIRS MINISTER LLOYD
AXWORTHY RESPONDED BY ENCOURAGING CASTRO TO LIGHTEN UP
AND REFLECT ON THE WARM WELCOME THE CUBANS RECEIVED
AT THE OPENING CEREMONY.

Norm Lourenco

Dan Galbraith

THRILL OF VICTORY & AGONY OF DEFEAT

From the promising beginning to the bitter end the Canadian men's baseball team
wore their hearts on their sleeves. They embodied Winnipeg's Pan Am Games in a
word: pride. For ten days of pure sporting entertainment, in one of the coziest baseball parks in the world, Canada's boys of summer were ambassadors for all that is good
about events like the Pan Am Games.

Early in the first week of competition, the country was bubbling with pride after
Canada out-dueled the American squad at their own game. It was a never-ending bat-
tle as leads changed hands and tempers flared. But that paled in comparison to
Canada's 11th inning heroics, rallying for three runs to tie and then adding the win-

76

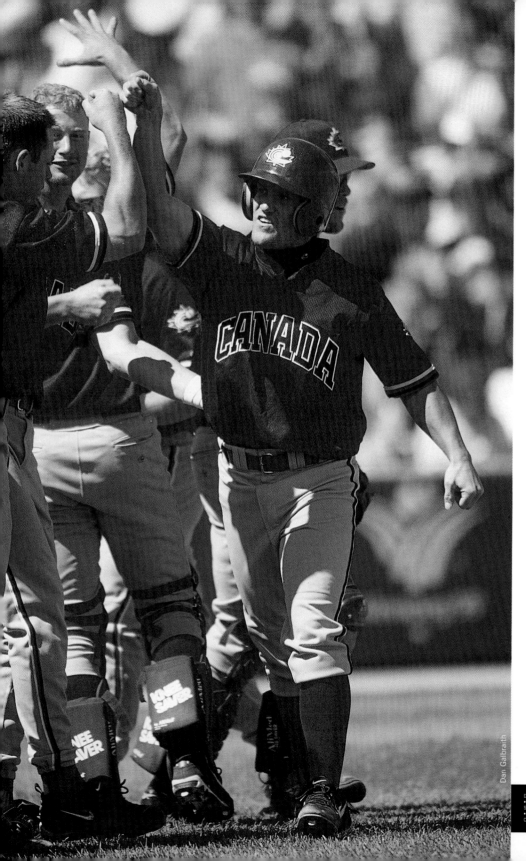

ner before three were out. It was a Hollywood movie-maker's dream come true: Canada down by three, their manager ejected from the game, the handsome catcher steps up to the plate and fulfills his boyhood fantasy. "I remember thinking to myself as I walked up to the plate," recalled Andy Stewart "that this was my chance, a once-in-a-lifetime opportunity." Stewart cranked the ball over the fence to tie it at six. Same inning, bases re-stocked, second baseman Stubby Clapp bloops one into left to make it a 7-6 final for Canada. Life may never be the same for a ballplayer from Windsor, Ontario named Stubby Clapp.

Canada's team was made up of mostly young minor-league professionals complemented with seven senior league players. They had no ties to the major leagues and they will never play together as a team again. "This was the closest most of us will ever get to the major leagues," confided Clapp. "I'm going to remember this for a long time." Clapp quickly became the talk of the Games and a huge fan-favourite. The crowd would roar whenever Clapp's name was pounded out by game announcers. Stubby was everywhere. Even the East Coast band The Great Big Sea, during a perfor-mance at the Forks, dedicated a song to "the one and only, Stubby Clapp." Clapp's legal first name is Richard, but Stubby is third generation in his family.

Cuba crashed the Canadians' cinderella party by handing Canada a heart-breaking semi-final 3-2 loss, eliminating them from gold-medal contention and a spot in the Sydney Olympics. It was their only loss of the tournament. Just two teams from the Americas will

Dan Galbraith

compete in Australia in 2000; a fact of baseball life that didn't seem fair in a tournament filled with so many talented teams and athletes from countries rich in baseball tradition. In their final game of the tournament, Canada beat Mexico to earn the bronze medal. The Canadians embraced the honour of being the first Canadian baseball team to ever win a Pan Am medal. "You just gotta take the moment and realize how special it really is," declared pitcher Jason Gooding.

DIAMOND MAGIC

If three times is a charm, a six-peat must be pure magic. And with that magic may finally come the respect that the Canadian men's softball program deserves. In defeating the United States in the gold-medal game at the John Blumberg Softball Complex, Canada extended its golden haul to six consecutive Pan Am tournaments. The 1999 squad holds the unique distinction of being the only team of the six to go undefeated (8-0) throughout the Games. "That's special," assured team coach Terry Baytor. "One of the hardest things to do is to win a competition in front of your home crowd. But our guys thrived on it. This was their World Series and they rose to the occasion."

Although it was war on the field between the two North American softball teams, there were few enemies among them. Many of the players are teammates on club teams, mainly south of the border. "I hit my roommate with a pitch," said Canada's Jody Hennigar slyly. "I'm sure he'll get me back next time we're on the road together."

The Canadian women's softball team was no less impressive. Although their Pan Am experience ended with a silver lining, they stole the hearts of thousands of delirious softball fans. Despite a 1-0 heartbreaking loss to the unconquerable U.S. team, there was nothing but pride and joy among the young, and relatively inexperienced women softballers. They nearly accomplished the impossible by pushing Team USA, the reigning world champions, past seven scoreless innings and into extra frames. Armed with the world's best pitchers, the American team yielded only one run in the entire tournament. The American women have not been beaten in international play since 1983, and have remained virtually intact since winning Olympic gold in Atlanta in 1996. The last team to beat them? Team Canada upset them with a 5-4 gold-medal victory at the Pan Am Games in Venezuela.

Don Gaudette

In the gold medal match, the men's field hockey team won a thriller. A heart-stopping 1-0 win over Argentina brought not only the gold, but an Olympic berth at the 2000 Olympics in Sydney - the first field hockey Olympic berth in eleven years.

FIELD HOCKEY

O R I G I N S Stick and ball games are among the oldest games on record. A drawing on an Egyptian tomb shows players using curved sticks to push around a small ball. Field hockey, believed to have descended from the Irish game of hurling, began to be organized in England in the mid-1800s. Women first played in 1887. The word "hockey" may originate from the French "hoquet", which is a shepherd's crooked staff.

FIELD OF DREAMS

Ask them who is the better field hockey player and they'll laugh, probably at the same time. What else would you expect from a couple who plays the same sport at the same high level of competition? Lisa Faust and Rick Roberts are both national team field hockey players. Married last year after competing at the World Cup in Holland, they walked out under an arch of field hockey sticks from the Dutch chapel where the ceremony was performed. Competing in their second Pan Ams as a couple (their first since making it legal) both are going home with a little extra baggage.

The men's team defeated Argentina to take the gold medal and the women outlasted Trinidad and Tobago to win the bronze. Captain of the women's squad, Faust was jubilant after her team's victory. "It was the last game of the tournament and we don't really know what the future holds for our team beyond these Games," explained Faust. "We were going to enjoy it." Faust admitted that the win may have been especially sweet for her because the couple had the chance to share their experiences. "Although, it was a little strange to be housed down the hall from each other," she confessed.

Dan Galbraith

Don Gaudette

VOLUNTEERS

Dan Galbraith

VOLUNTEERS

Dan Galbraith

EQUESTRIAN

O R I G I N S Horses have been used extensively throughout history for transportation and in farming, hunting and the military. Equestrian competitors use many of the skills of hunters and soldiers on horseback. The three-day event originated within the cavalry to test the versatility, obedience, endurance and jumping ability of both horse and rider. Prior to 1950, Canada fielded a military equestrian team. Canada has won four Olympic medals and four world championship medals since it first took part in the Olympics in 1952.

Lady luck showered veteran Canadian Olympic show jumper Ian Millar with gold on the final day of competition. In the 52-year-old's final five knuckle-biting, nerve-wrack-

VOLUNTEERS

Dan Galbraith

ing rides, the seasoned champ rode three fault-free. The final top three riders knocked down jumps, leaving Millar and Ivar, his nine-year-old gelding, the surprise winners to the delight of five thousand screaming partisan spectators. "The Canadian gods intervened," noted one American observer.

Millar has more medals than anyone on the Canadian equestrian team, a feat that has earned him the Order of Canada and an induction into Canada's Sports Hall of Fame. Millar's medals include double gold at the 1987 Pan Ams, three team silvers from 1979, 1983 and 1991 and an individual bronze in the 1979 Pan Am Games. He has competed in seven Olympiads, capturing one Olympic medal - a team gold in 1980 in Rotterdam, the year of the boycott of the Moscow Games.

SPORT OF KINGS

We may be living in modern times but the ancient sport of kings still draws a crowd. Dressage, the least popular but by far the most formal of the three equestrian events, is likened to ballet for horses. Riders are dressed in black frock coats with tails, top hats and gloves while horses, decked out in tightly-braided manes prance and step to elegantly choreographed routines. Dressage began as a method of training horses and officers for warfare. Horses were trained to simultaneously move forward and sideways - even pirouette - to perfect skills vital in sidestepping cannonballs and arrows during battle in the Middle Ages. The second of the trio of equestrian events is called eventing, a three-day endurance test which includes dressage, a steeplechase and a cross-country race. The final event of the equestrian competition is show jumping, where the rider's skill, and the horse's jumping ability and speed, are tested over a course of obstacles. Equestrian events are complex to organize. Many of the horses are worth more than one million dollars and arrive at venues with near-regal entourages. Horses are not exempt from dope testing.

VOLUNTEERS

Norm Lourenco

TRACK & FIELD

O R I G I N S The origins of a number of athletics events date back to ancient Greece. The discus throw and various running events, for example, were part of the ancient Olympics. The marathon was introduced at the 1896 Athens Olympics, the first Games of the modern era, in honour of the ancient Greek soldier Pheidippides. According to the legend, he ran from Marathon to Athens with news of a Greek victory over the Persians, then died from exhaustion. Events such as the pole vault may have originated with European farmers who used long poles to help them vault over ditches. And naval gunners hefting cannonballs may have been the originators of the shotput.

85

CRISIS FOR CUBA

Crisis for Cuba at the University of Manitoba track. Gold-medal high jumper Javier Sotomayer failed doping, testing positive for cocaine. Sotomayer denied using the drug and the Cuban delegation charged that persons unknown, or at least unnamed, had spiked his food or drink. Only days earlier the woman's gold-medal high jumper, Dominican Juana Rosario, was also stripped of her medal for a doping failure - in her case a banned steroid - and too denied taking the drug. Sotomayor's test meant double gold medals for Canada - Mark Boswell and Kwaku Boateng had made identical silver-medal jumps and, in less than ideal fashion, moved up to gold.

Dan Galbraith

Dan Galbraith

Dan Galbraith

Dan Galbraith

TINY ISLAND MAKES HISTORY IN WINNIPEG

As the United States, Cuba and Canada battled it out for the medal count lead at the Pan Am Games, a tiny island country of 40,000, no bigger than 100 square miles, celebrated its first major international medal. Kareem Streete-Thompson's silver in the men's long jump was the first medal ever for the Cayman Islands at a Pan Am Games, Commonwealth Games, Olympics or a world championship.

Accustomed to sending only small teams to even the largest of international events - the country itself has fewer residents than Portage la Prairie and Brandon combined - Streete-Thompson's medal is a watershed that has been a long time coming. The team's chef de mission

V O L U N T E E R S

Norm Lourenco

Dan Galbraith

immediately phoned home to the tiny three-island nation, waking up the country's director of sports with the news that Streete-Thompson had won. By the time all the phone calls were done, hundreds of sports officials in the Cayman Islands knew: they had their first medal.

LIFE IN THE FAST LANE

Graham Hood saw gold and his parents. Donovan Bailey was looking for redemption. Both found what they were after at the finish line.

Winnipeg-born Hood, electrified the capacity crowd at the University of Manitoba Stadium on the track and field competition's final evening, with a brilliant kick to capture gold in the men's 1,500-metre final. The 27-year-old Torontonian had a plan: Keep with the pack for 1,400

VOLUNTEERS

metres and then bolt around the final turn. But Hood had not accounted for the throng of fans who began to mount a roar as he found his feet and started to slice through the field in the backstretch of the final lap. As he came down the home stretch, Hood could make out his parents jumping up and down in the stands amid a sea of Canadian flags and fans. He then simply switched gears and no one would catch him ... an evening he'll remember for a long time to come.

So too will the capacity crowd that witnessed Bailey's explosion out of the blocks in the men's 4x100 metre relay. His sprint sparked the Canadian quartet to a silver medal, behind the speedy Brazilians who captured gold with a Games record time of 38.18 seconds.

Bailey, still recovering from a torn Achilles tendon suffered last fall and a turbulent week of controversy in Winnipeg surrounding his poster boy turned bad boy involvement with the Games, caught up to both runners ahead of him in the staggered start, giving Canada a commanding first-leg lead. The team's final time: 38:49.

Canada added two more athletics medals that last night when Kwaku Boateng and Mark Boswell won silvers - which later became golds as a result of the winner's positive dope test - in the men's high-jump after posting identical leaps of 2.25 metres. The Canadian track and field team collected 14 medals in total, a marked improvement from the six garnered at the 1995 Pan Am Games. Other highlights from the athletics competition included the gold-medal run in the 3,000-metre steeplechase by New Brunswick's Joel Bourgeois, and Leah Pells' breath-stopping photo finish silver in the women's 1,500 metre.

Phil Hossack

Wayne Glowacki

Keith Levit

TO RUN OR NOT TO RUN

In the eyes of many Pan Am Games enthusiasts, Donovan Bailey arrived in Winnipeg a day late and a race short. Bailey, the defending Olympic gold medallist and former world record holder, found himself at the center of a turbulent week-long storm of criticism that died a quiet death the night he took to the podium as an integral part of the silver-medal relay team. In days previous, Bailey was caught in the crossfire of spectator and athlete convictions targeted at his refusal of an offer from Athletics Canada to run the 100-metre showcase event because he was not asked earlier than he was. Initially, Bailey failed to qualify for the event when he placed third at the qualifier. But Bruny Surin, occupant of one of Canada's two berths in the competition, made little effort to hide his lack of enthusiasm for the Pan Ams. When Surin gave up his spot to compete elsewhere, Bailey would not accept the "alternate" invitation citing lack of preparation as the reason for his decision. The Pan Am community's contentions were fueled by Bailey's receipt of more than $200,000 from Winnipeg's Pan Am organizing committee to promote the Games during the final year leading up to the event. In his own defense, Bailey suggested that the Pan Am organizers understood his predicament where the selection process was concerned, and were happy with what he had done for the Games.

VOLUNTEERS

Norm Lourenco

MAN, WOMAN & MACHINE

CYCLING

O R I G I N S Bicycle racing is as old as the bicycle, which was developed in the 19th century. One of the most popular early designs was the penny-farthing bicycle, so-named because of its huge front wheel and tiny rear wheel. These machines were also called "boneshakers", and their design made them inherently unstable. The fore-runner of today's bicycles, called the "safety" bicycle, was developed in the late 1800s. It led to a boom in competitive and recreational cycling. Competitive cycling has tra-ditionally consisted of road and track events, but the rise in popularity in recent years of all-terrain bicycles has led to a third discipline, mountain biking, being added to

92

Dan Galbraith

games programs internationally. Women's events were only recently added to the Olympic program, road in 1984 and track in 1988. At the Pan Am Games, entries are restricted to a total of six women per country.

TANYA'S GAMES

These were Tanya's games. Tanya Dubnicoff, the 26-year-old cyclist who carried the Canadian flag at the Opening Ceremony, cycled to two gold medals. But there was more to it than that. She constantly smiled and obliged; she cheerfully did countless interviews and she went out of her way to promote the Pan Am Games. And she did it for nothing. "She breathed more life into these Games than any other individual," said Mayor Glen Murray. "She was incredible."

VOLUNTEERS

Dan Galbraith

HEART OF GOLD

If Pan Am medals were struck for the athlete with the biggest heart and the biggest smile, Winnipeg's Clara Hughes would have walked away with gold in both categories. Unfortunately, the 26-year-old finished both of her cycling road races below her expectations and out of the medals. But she was first with the fans, her teammates and the reporters who followed her everywhere. Her friendly, shy demeanor and the big smile permanently stamped on her freckled face even in defeat, earned her the unofficial title of "Sweetheart of the Games."

Norm Lourenco

94

Norm Lourenco

VOLUNTEERS

Norm Lourenco

Hughes, a double bronze medallist at the 1996 Olympics, had battled injuries for several years and weary of the constant struggle to come back, retired briefly from competitive cycling in 1998. She wanted to say good-bye to a sport that had won her world recognition. "A year before the Pan Ams I was at the Winnipeg Folk Festival with a cast on my leg and I didn't think I'd ever race my bike again," Hughes remembered. She could have stayed away from the Games, but that's not what home-town heroes do. Especially when it means representing Canada in your home town. "Just being here for the people, and showing them that a Winnipeg girl can compete at this level, it's special," she offered proudly.

97

VOLUNTEERS

ROWING

ORIGINS   A boat powered by oars is one of the simplest and oldest forms of water transportation. Rowing as sport, as opposed to a means of transport, goes back to ancient times. Virgil mentions a boat race in the *Aeneid*. The modern form of the sport developed in England in the late 18th and early 19th centuries. One of the earliest recorded races is the sculling race for "Doggett's Coat and Badge," first held in 1715. One of the key technological developments that helped further the sport was the outrigger, which enabled the oars to be "rigged out" from the side of the boat, therefore making it possible to build a narrower and faster boat. Until the invention of the sliding seat in 1857, oarsmen used leather pants and axle grease to slide back and forth easily on their seats. Professional Canadian scullers, including Ned Hanlan, dominated the international scene in the late 1800s. Rowing has traditionally been a strong sport for Canada, especially in recent years.

HERE'S TO YOU EMMA ROBINSON
Emma Robinson's golden come-back is complete. Four months after surgery for thyroid cancer, the Winnipeg rower brought home Pan Am gold at Lake Minnedosa, as she and pairs partner Theresa Luke powered gracefully past the competition. "It makes me feel proud to be able to compete at home," Robinson expressed after she and Luke finished eight seconds ahead of Americans Karen Kraft and Missy Ryan to the cheers of Robinson's flag-draped parents and friends.

Dan Galbraith

Dan Galbraith

"I'm really happy to be here and I'm happy that things seem to be fully recovered." Robinson's determination to resume training within days of surgery and radiation treatment inspired Luke of 100 Mile House, B.C., to achieve her best as well. "I'm able to say, 'Wow, if she can do that, I can do that and more.'" Other than a few days when she had to stay away from her teammates because she was radioactive, Robinson said health problems have not affected her training. The type of thyroid cancer Robinson

SHARP WORDS Marnie McBean, the world-class rower, said what a lot of people were thinking - that she had had it with Donovan Bailey's sulking and wished the Pan Am Games had spent its $200,000 promotional fund on someone more deserving. Bailey's nose was out of joint because he was not invited to run the 100-metre event after finishing third in the trials. Bailey refused to be called up as an alternate. "Donovan should have been a little more patient and maybe a bit more humble waiting for an invitation," said McBean.

VOLUNTEERS

faced is much more treatable than most cancers, giving her a 95 per cent chance of surviving at least another five years.

"On the one hand, you feel really grateful but ... that's her life we're talking about," said Emma's mother, Maureen, who hugged and kissed her daughter repeatedly after the golden race. The athlete said cancer made her pay more attention to the world outside of rowing, but it also reaffirmed her decision to take a two-year leave from medical school to train for the Sydney Olympics.

Not particularly athletic themselves, Emma's parents had no idea how much work it takes to become a world-class athlete until their daughter started getting up at the crack of dawn every day, Maureen admitted. But she put her new insights to good use during the Pan Am Games as coordinator of counselling services at the University of Manitoba's athlete village.

CHAIRMAN OF THE OARS

The chairman of the Pan Am Games committee flew into Lake Minnedosa to take in some of the rowing competition and to relive a moment from his adolescence. Sandy Riley was a 16-year-old boat holder for rowing events held on the Winnipeg floodway during the 1967 Pan Am Games, an experience that changed his life, as he told countless people preparing for this year's Games. Riley, now president of Investors Group, held a shell for the Peruvian lightweight men's quad crew from the starting dock until the start was called. "The trick is not to fall in the water," he laughed, explaining that the docks are designed for kids who weigh about 100 lbs.

Dan Galbraith

VOLUNTEERS

Manuel F. Sousa

101

VOLUNTEERS

Norm Lourenco

Norm Lourenco

SAILING

O R I G I N S When the invention of sails made it possible to move across water without rowing, many different types of vessels and arrangements of sails were developed throughout the world, depending on the climate and the user's needs. The name yacht comes from the Dutch "jachtschip," meaning "hunting ship," because these small, fast vessels were originally developed for hunting pirates. The speed and manoeuverability of yachts also made them ideal for sport. King Charles II of England was an early proponent of yachting - he initially used a small navy vessel for sport and pleasure, then had several more built for racing. A sport of the aristocracy in its early days, yachting has become gradually more accessible to people, particularly through the development of building materials such as marine plywood and resin glues.

VOLUNTEERS

Norm Lourenco

LIKE FATHER, LIKE SON

The youngest competitor in the Pan Am sailing races on Lake Winnipeg had a very important job in the eyes of his skipper. Juan Maegli Aguero and son Juan Maegli Novella teamed up in the Hobie Cat 16 event, with father at the helm and son keeping an eye on the competition while handling the jib on the catamaran. The father and son team have sailed together for five years. Juan is just 11 years old but his father said he's the best crew he could have. The duo carries on a family tradition of sailing in the big leagues. Juan the elder sailed with his father in the 1971 Pan American Games.

Norm Lourenco

VOLUNTEERS

Dan Galbraith

WATER SKIING

O R I G I N S The development of small motorboats led inevitably to the development of water skiing. Over the past 40 years, water skiing has evolved from a "cottage" leisure activity into a sophisticated sport. An estimated 2.5 million Canadians currently water ski recreationally, which makes for a large base from which to draw elite level

104

skiers. Having won numerous titles over the years, Canadian water skiers are recognized as some of the best in the world.

INVENTIVE TRICKSTERS

Alberta brothers Jaret and Kreg Llewellyn are international stars in the water ski world. They have had a major impact on their sport by way of child's play. A game they invented as kids while water skiing in Innisfail, Alberta, has been recognized as an official trick, or figure, component of international water skiing. The ski-line "540 trick" requires skiers to jump over the tow rope, spin around 540 degrees and jump back over again. The Llewellyn's 540 has been incorporated into a series of quick tricks the skiers perform in a 20-second span.

ONE LAST SPLASH

It was the most spectacular jump of the day but one Canada's Jim Clunie wished he could do over again. Making his final pass in the water skiing jump preliminaries, Clunie lost his grip on the bar and cart-wheeled into the water in front of 1,950 spectators. The crowd was stunned at the sight of what appeared to be the

VOLUNTEERS

Dan Galbraith

event's first serious injury and waited breathlessly for what seemed like an eternity before Clunie surfaced and waved, signaling he was okay. Clunie was traveling almost 100 kilometres an hour with an 800-pound force pulling on the tow bar when he hit the ramp. It's a wonder that he and other skiers, can hold onto the bar at all. The injury wasn't serious. His previous jump, sixth best of the day, qualified him for the next day's final.

The little-known Clunie has been a staple on the international water skiing circuit for the past ten years, jumping in water ski competitions around the world. "If you win you can make about $6,000 but if you finish in the top six you can at least pay your expenses," Clunie explained. As a youngster, Clunie got hooked on water skiing when he realized there wasn't much room in the National Hockey League for a 5-4 left-

Dan Galbraith

Dan Galbraith

winger. He quit school at the age of 16 and moved to the central Florida community of Okahumpka to attend the internationally renowned Jack Travers Ski School.

The Pan Am Games was his first competition of the year and the last of his career. Retiring to take on the role of sales manager for his family's trucking company, Kelsey Trail Trucking, he was hoping to go out with a bang. Maybe not the bang he gave to the spectators, but a final performance he knows he still has inside him. "Sometimes when something like this happens, you come out and ski harder the next day," Clunie professed. "I'm ready for one last time."

VOLUNTEERS

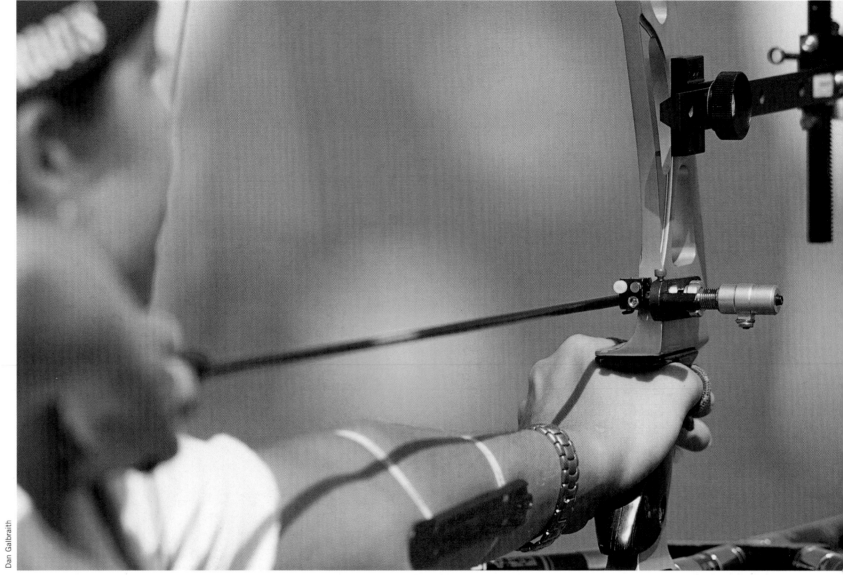

Dan Galbraith

TAKING AIM

ARCHERY

O R I G I N S Bows and arrows have been important weapons of hunting and war since their invention 50,000 years ago. With the advent of firearms, they became obsolete as weapons but archery continued to be practiced as a target sport. A new

VOLUNTEERS

Dan Galbraith

Dan Galbraith

spectator-friendly format was introduced at the 1996 Olympics and was used for the 1999 Pan American Games. Unlike the former international competition environment that demanded silence from spectators, now the crowd is encouraged to cheer as the athletes compete against each other in head-to-head elimination rounds.

HITTING THE MARK

The new format for Pan Am archery seemed to have been right on target. Winnipeg introduced elimination shoot-outs to replace the standard awarding of medals to the top scores over a period of days. The new approach created an exciting atmosphere, most notice-

VOLUNTEERS

Dan Galbraith

ably witnessed during an exhilarating men's team semi-final match in which the upstart Canadians defeated the experienced Cuban team.

A record-breaking final by the Americans didn't spoil the young Canadian archers' spirits, as they drew back, aimed at gold and shot for silver. "We were really pumped," enthused Rob Rusnov, the team senior at age 25 and the only member of

VOLUNTEERS

Dan Galbraith

Dan Galbraith

the team with international competition experience. "Being in our own country made this an awesome time for all of us ... despite the added pressure," he enthused. Between shots, the Canadian archers would share in high-fives and whoop it up after each good arrow.

SHOOTING

O R I G I N S The ancient Chinese invented gunpowder, eventually revolutionizing warfare and hunting. Shooting festivals were held in northern Europe as early as the 16th century. Early firearms were notoriously inaccurate. The idea of rifling, or cutting spiral grooves inside the gun barrel (hence the name "rifle"), vastly increased the accuracy of firearms. Competitive shooting began in the late 18th century when

VOLUNTEERS

pistols replaced swords for dueling. Target shooting developed only after a number of technical advances made weapons more accurate. Competitions evolved to test a variety of weapons and targets.

SIGHT OF A LIFETIME

Bruce Meredith grew up with a rifle in his hand. Raised in the rural backwoods of West Virginia, guns were a necessity when running water was a luxury. He attended a military high school on a work scholarship: "I washed dishes and cut meat during lunch hour to earn my keep at the school," recalls Meredith. "The reward came in the form of a once-a-week mandatory marksmanship class." Meredith quickly earned the distinction of being the most successful shooter in his class. To nurture his talent he pursued a university that offered courses in shooting.

Dan Galbraith

Money was an object however. Meredith couldn't afford to go to post-secondary school until a year-long stint at a steel mill provided the means to attend the University of West Virginia, with its reputable shooting team. Four years later Meredith graduated with honours in rifle shooting - he was the national champion. A job in the military provided him with the opportunity to represent his country at the Pan Am Games in 1967.

His keen eye and steady hand have served him well over more than three decades. Meredith has taken aim at six Pan Am Games, three Olympic Games and five World Championships. Thirty-two years after his gold medal performance in Winnipeg, the 62-year-old retired U.S. Army Colonel, who now represents the U.S. Virgin Islands, sat in the very gun range where it all began and reflected. "I'm out to have fun now; I've been there when the pressure's on and nothing but a win will do. It's relaxation time now," he pledged.

Although medals no longer come as readily for the pistol and rifle shooter, Meredith is not ready to lock up the guns and call it quits just yet. He admits that his vision is not as acute as it used to be, his training isn't as intense and his promises to his wife about slowing down are soon to be more rigorously enforced. "But will you see me in future competitions?" Meredith questioned rhetorically. "You can count on it."

VOLUNTEERS

Keith Levit

TENPIN BOWLING

O R I G I N S Bowling is an ancient game. Nine marble pins and several small stones discovered in an ancient Egyptian child's tomb place its origins as far back as 5200 B.C. The game has been a popular recreational activity and sport in Canada since the early 1900s. Canadians may be more familiar with the five-pin version of bowling, invented by Torontonian Tommy Ryan in 1909. Bowling alleys were an exclusively male domain for many years, which meant that when Marian Sutherland broke with tradition and bowled a public game in Toronto in 1916, she made headlines.

T H E B O W L I N G S E B E L E N F A M I L Y Rolando Sebelen lowered the camcorder, his face flush with pride. "Not too many people can say they participate in sport at this level," the 59-year-old Dominican smiled, "but I'm also lucky to be on the same team as my sons." Sebelen was videotaping his sons Rolly and Rolando Antonio Sebelen bowling in the masters qualifying round of the Pan Am Games tenpin competition at Club Laverendrye.

The three Sebelens, all named Rolando, bowl on the four-man Dominican Republic team, where a mutual admiration between father and sons exists. "He's a very competitive athlete," boasted Rolly, Rolando's 35-year-old namesake. "He pushes us, because he always does his best."

Papa Sebelen is a former world champion who has rolled four perfect games in his career, a total matched

113

by Rolando Antonio, the youngest at 31 years old. The family has the luxury of honing their skills at their own bowling alley in the Dominican Republic, the Sebelen Bowling Centre in Santo Domingo, the only bowling facility on the tropical island. With the 2003 Pan Am Games slated for their city of two million, the future hosts of the tenpin bowling event are impressed with Winnipeg's spirit. "Winnipeg has had great organization, and everyone's so friendly," said Rolly. "We will have to do our best to match Winnipeg's efforts."

"God gave me the chance to bowl with my boys," offered Rolando proudly, who is looking forward to the upcoming bowling world championships in the United Arab Emirates, where third son, 25-year-old Rolando Rafael, will join the team. "We have to make the most of these chances." And there's a chance for more Rolando magic in the future. "I have a five-year-old son, same name as me, back home who bowls," said Rolando Antonio. "To bowl with him and my father would be extra special."

Ruth Bonneville

VOLUNTEERS

Dan Galbraith

IN THE POOL

DIVING

O R I G I N S The origins of diving go back to the first person who came to a high place overlooking a deep pool of water and decided to dive in. Mexicans and Polynesians in particular took advantage of their landscape to become skilled divers. Even ancient Vikings were known to practice cliff diving. The Swedes and Germans helped launch modern competitive diving when they developed "fancy diving", using gymnastics equipment to add somersaults and twists to their dives. Early competitions were recorded in the 1880s in Germany and Scotland.

Dan Galbraith

115

VOLUNTEERS

Dan Galbraith

Dan Galbraith

SWIMMING

O R I G I N S Although not part of the ancient Olympic Games, swimming was included in the training of ancient Greek and Roman soldiers. It was not favoured as a competitive or recreational activity in medieval Europe, but became popular there in the 19th century. Swimming competitions were held in Japan as early as 36 B.C. An imperial edict there even made it a compulsory part of the school curriculum in 1603. Early swimming competitors did not have the benefit of today's modern pools; swimming competitions were held in any available water. Events at the first modern Olympics in 1896, for example, were held in choppy ocean water. Four years later Olympic swimmers raced down the Seine River in Paris.

VOLUNTEERS

Dan Galbraith

A RECORD MEDAL HAUL

The Canadian swim team made a spectacular splash at the pool from the competition's start to its finish. The 32-member team surfaced from the six-day competition with 32 medals in all - three more than their best performances at the 1967 and 1975 Pan Am Games. Vancouver's Jessica Deglau led the way with four gold medals and two silvers, establishing the eighteen-year-old butterfly ace as the most decorated Canadian swimmer ever at a Pan Am Games.

Dan Galbraith

VOLUNTEERS

SYNCHRONIZED SWIMMING

ORIGINS While there is evidence of swimmers performing ballet-like manoeuvers in the water in ancient times, the origin of synchronized swimming as an organized, competitive sport dates back to earlier this century. In the 1920s, a group of Canadian women, led by national caliber water polo player and diver Margaret Sellers, developed what they called "ornamental swimming" from life saving and swimming techniques. Over the next 20 years the sport grew, music was added to the routines and the name changed to "synchronized swimming." Canadians have continued to be leaders in developing the sport. The inaugural world championships were held in 1973, and the sport first appeared on the Olympic Games program in 1984. Canada has won medals at all four Olympics to date.

CHOREOGRAPHY, GRACE & GOLD

On the Games' final weekend of competition, the Canadian synchronized swimming team shed their perennial second-place status with a sweet victory over the top-ranked Americans in the free team event. For years, Canada's synchronized swimmers have been relegated to second best behind the Americans in every major international synchro competition. Even before the winners were announced, hundreds of Canadian flag-waving spectators - anticipating gold for Canada - erupted in a chorus of cheers and unrestrained joy after the American team finished its routine with a score just a fraction below Canada's mark.

Dan Galbraith

Canada's performance, based on the theme of time and the dawning of the new millennium drew thunderous applause from the crowd as the eight-member team swam to victory with stunning form, agility and precision. In fact, it was the electricity generated by the audience's overwhelming support that team member Lesley Wright credits as a major factor in the win. The native of Saskatoon explained that the team fed off of that energy. "Before we were even introduced, everyone was screaming and cheering; we could see our families and the Canadian flags flying. It just fills you up."

Dan Galbraith

Dan Galbraith

WATER POLO

O R I G I N S Water polo began during the 1860s as entertainment during British swimming competitions. Players would mount apple barrels and manoeuver through the water to try to get a ball in a net. These "water derby" players would continue the game from the water if they got thrown from the barrels. The game gradually changed from entertainment into a fast-paced, exciting water sport. Until some of the rules were changed to limit body contact, water polo games could also be quite rough. Even today, competitive players wear two bathing suits because they stand a good chance of losing one during the course of a game. This was the first time women's water polo had been on the Pan American Games program and it makes its Olympic debut at the 2000 Games in Sydney.

V O L U N T E E R S

PROUD CANADIANS

The Canadian men's water polo team need no longer wonder how to attract the attention of the entire country to their sport. The fervent squad landed squarely in the spotlight during the Opening Ceremony and subsequently was the talk of the town for days to follow. After all of the athletes from the participating nations paraded into Winnipeg Stadium, members of the men's water polo team broke away from the Canadian contingent during their proud stroll. A deafening roar erupted when the young mavericks produced a giant Canada Flag and proceeded to race it around the Stadium.

"We smuggled the flag in," confessed Darryl Bourne, a Winnipegger and the captain of the team. "One of the guys put it in his pants," he laughed. Bourne was ecstatic after he and his mates left the pack and took flight. "It was the biggest rush in the world. It was better than I ever imagined. My heart was pounding," admitted a shameless Bourne. "Just as we were coming through the tunnel, everyone started chanting 'Canada, Canada, Canada!' I didn't know 40,000 people could make that much noise."

The water polo team made front page news in papers across the country the next morning. Despite warnings

Dan Galbraith

VOLUNTEERS

Dan Galbraith

from Canadian team officials, the patriotic crew decided to go ahead with the plan anyway. "We wear our hearts on our sleeves and this is something everyone will remember," stated Bourne unapologetically. "We have national pride and that's something we as Canadians sometimes don't show as much as we should."

Bourne realized the water polo team's unabashed stunt stole the show. They respected that it was Tanya Dubnicoff's moment to shine as team flag-bearer and didn't intend to steal her thunder. "We didn't want to take anything away from Tanya. She gave us the thumbs up after we were seated so we knew what we did was well received by everyone."

Maybe they were inspired by their win in the water earlier that day or maybe it was just the excitement of the Games. But whatever it was that prompted them, their spirit created a wave of emotion throughout the stadium, rippling into the souls of television viewers nationwide. These men may not have won the gold medal that they came to Winnipeg to claim but they won the hearts of the fans, which Bourne felt was worth more than gold.

THE WOMEN'S WATER POLO TEAM OUTPLAYED THE U.S. TO TAKE THE GOLD MEDAL. AS THE WOMEN RECEIVED THEIR MEDALS TO THE SOUNDS OF O' CANADA, THE TEAM GAVE A CHORUS LINE BOW, A REMINDER THAT WATER ISN'T ALWAYS FROZEN FOR GREAT CANADIAN SPORTING MOMENTS. THE MEN'S TEAM, BOUNCING BACK FROM THEIR OVERTIME LOSS TO CUBA, BEAT BRAZIL FOR BRONZE IN OVERTIME WITH WINNIPEGGER DARRYL BOURNE FIRING THE WINNING GOAL.

VOLUNTEERS

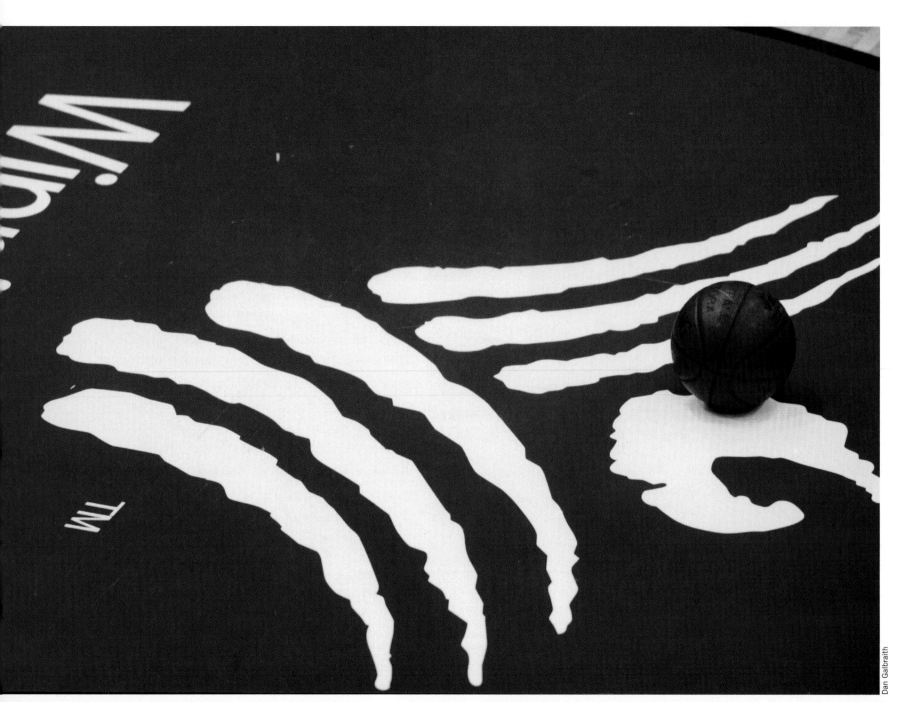

Dan Galbraith

VOLUNTEERS

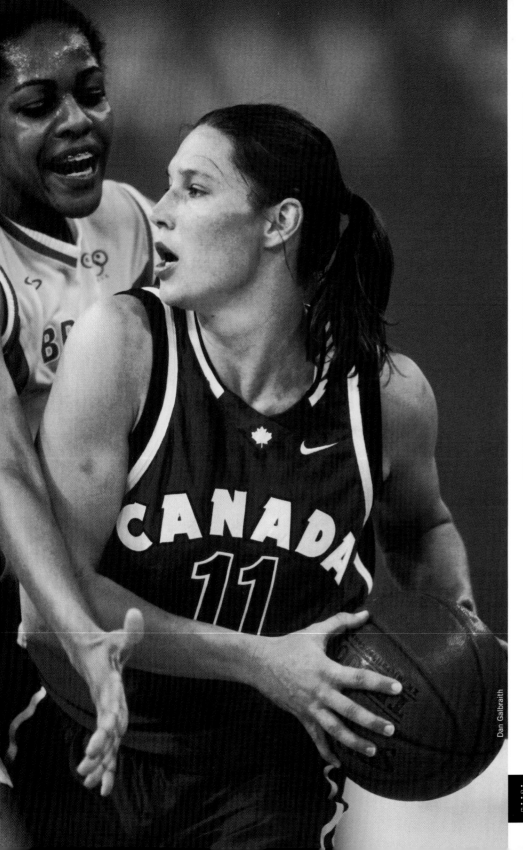

Dan Galbraith

ON THE COURT

BASKETBALL

O R I G I N S Basketball was invented in 1891 by Canadian James Naismith as a way of keeping youth busy while they were waiting for the baseball season to start. The first players used peach baskets nailed to the wall and a soccer ball. The new game caught on quickly, and by 1936 had become an official Olympic sport. The Canadian team won the first silver medal. The first women's Olympic basketball tournament was held in Montreal in 1976.

BRAZILIANS CROWNED KINGS OF THE COURT

It does not matter where the tournament is held, there is always one constant in international basketball: It sure feels good to beat the United States. The Brazilian men's basketball team experienced a taste of that winning feeling when they overthrew the U.S. 95-78 to capture gold.

When the final buzzer sounded, Brazil's entire team ran over to the stands and joined in a frantic song and dance number with their boisterous fans. The relentless cheering section provided a game-long soundtrack of cheers for their countrymen and jeers for their opponents. "This win, it is a very special occasion," explained Brazil's head coach Helio Rubens.

The U.S. was undefeated going into the gold-medal game. The squad featured a line-up of Continental Basketball Association stars who had been together only three weeks before the tournament commenced. U.S. head coach Mo McHone noted that the lack of preparation was key to his team's loss, but was quick to pay tribute to the outstanding display of shooting by Brazil.

On the other side of the court, Brazil is trying to rebuild its men's basketball program after losing many of its top players to retirement in recent years. Brazil's failure to qualify for the Olympics in 2000 at an earlier tournament put much emphasis on winning the Pan Am gold medal to re-establish their reputation in the region. With its victory, Brazil demonstrated once again that international basketball has improved dramatically.

VOLUNTEERS

Dan Galbraith

Norm Lourenco

FIGHTING HER OWN BATTLE

One year before the Games began, Nancy Lee Karpinsky wasn't thinking about Pan Am gold - she was trying to stay alive. A member of the Canadian women's handball team, Karpinsky has Crohn's Disease. The intestinal affliction kept her in a Montreal hospital bed for three weeks. The 5-foot-8 Karpinsky weighed only 118 pounds at that point, almost 30 pounds less than her playing weight. The 26-year-old Winnipegger described herself as "skin and bones", and harboured little hope for a return to the handball team.

Doctors told her to rest. But Karpinsky knew the clock was ticking on her Pan Am dream, so she headed out to the national team's practice. She was supposed to just watch but soon joined in a sit-up here and a push-up there. With the help of her teammates, slowly her muscle came back and so did her spirits. Karpinsky competed in Winnipeg to the delight of her family and friends. Although her team's dream for gold and a coveted berth in the 2000 Olympics in Sydney died, Karpinsky's hopes for a handball career are alive and well. She intends to play semi-pro in France for a year before finishing off her education degree. And aside from a sprained thumb and Achilles tendinitis in her feet, Karpinsky herself is alive and well.

TEAM HANDBALL

O R I G I N S Team handball developed around the turn of the century as an adaptation of soccer. It was first played on a soccer field with the rules modified to suit moving the ball with the hands. The rules changed again to adapt the game to indoor play. Originally intended for girls because it was considered improper for them to play soccer, the game quickly became popular with both men and women.

VOLUNTEERS

WHAT'S IN A GAME?

It was the game with no tomorrows. In what was one of the most emotional gold-medal finals of the Pan Am Games, Team Canada lost the gold medal, and their only opportunity to qualify for the Sydney Olympics, to Brazil in women's Team Handball.

In an extraordinarily aggressive match, the scoreboard's final 31-27 reading told the tale of converse emotions and futures. Canada's tear-streaked faces spoke of tragedy; Brazil's of jubilation.

"We tried our very best," choked out Nancy Lee Karpinsky, unsuccessful in her attempt to hold on to her composure. "We played with all our hearts. We knew that this was our last chance. We just lost to a better team," she added in the spirit of true sportsmanship.

The Canadian team had been training for the tournament for three years, but nothing could have prepared them for the emotional rollercoaster that the competition presented. Beating the tough U.S. squad, many of whom are team- or league-mates of the Canadians playing in Europe, was an incredibly highpoint of the Games as it put them in contention for the Olympic berth.

Tess Contos of Team USA insisted that the Team USA versus Team Canada competition was a friendly one. Spectators may offer a slightly different commentary after having watched the teams abuse each other throughout the entirety of both 30-minute halves. "On the court we're adversaries ... when we're off the court we support each other," she reiterated. "There's going to be disappointment on one side of the coin no

Norm Lourenco

Norm Lourenco

126

Norm Lourenco

matter who wins or loses. It would be awesome for the Canadians or the U.S. to get on the world's handball map."

Both teams left Winnipeg feeling dissatisfied. The Americans lost the bronze-medal game to Cuba and for Canada, second place just wasn't good enough. "We came here to win the gold. We worked for years to get to this game. We can be proud that we did the best we could. Maybe a little later silver will taste a little better," Karpinsky calculated carefully. "It's been a once-in-a-life-time opportunity ... a dream week. We did our best and that's all you can ask for," she concluded with the polish of a seasoned professional athlete.

Although relatively unknown in North America, handball is the third most popular sport in the world. European elite players enjoy the status of world-class athletes, making a comfortable living. On this side of the Atlantic, things aren't so easy for handball players. "The handball federation in both the U.S. and Canada are not well supported by the corporate community. "It's a catch-22," suggested Contos. "We need development but we don't have the money for development." Canadian Team members each paid $500 of their own money to prepare for the tournament.

"This game meant a lot, not only for us as a team, but for women's handball across Canada," declared Karpinsky. "There was a lot riding on not only winning but performing well. I think we can hold our heads high. There is a future for the sport in this country."

127

VOLUNTEERS

Dan Galbraith

VOLLEYBALL & BEACH VOLLEYBALL

O R I G I N S Volleyball was invented in 1895 by William Morgan, director of physical recreation at the YMCA in Holyoake, Massachusetts. He was looking for a game to be played by some of his students that was less strenuous than basketball, invented four years earlier. Volleyball started as a co-operative game, the object being to keep the ball in play as long as possible. The sport spread internationally as the YMCA movement flourished. Beach volleyball can be traced back to the late 1920s, when families could be found playing six-on-six on the beaches of California.

PRESSURE FRONT AND CENTER

The pressure to win fell squarely on the shoulders of each man on the team, but it was four players from the University of Manitoba who felt it most in Team Canada's quest for medal contention in men's volleyball. Playing for their University coach, Garth Pischke, in their university home-town, and without several veterans who opted for a couple of recuperation months in anticipation of upcoming competition-heavy Olympic qualifiers, Winnipeg's fabulous four could barely breathe.

Facing a tough Brazilian team in the semi-finals, Canada fought gallantly, but couldn't keep up the offensive pressure. Short lapses in routine service reception and poor net play gave the Brazilian team small windows of opportunity which they eagerly exploited. The powerful Brazilian offense capitalized and slowly converted a slim lead into a comfortable advantage. Though the Canadian team had the lion's share of support from the cacophonous crowd, the Brazilian cheering contingent was not to be outdone; their small numbers belied their infectious fervor. Their countrymen endured.

Team captain Brian Koskie explained his team's frustration. "Brazil is a very good team. As a team we knew we had to play our perfect game and I think we put a little too much pressure on ourselves. We made mistakes. You just can't make mistakes in this event. It was so disappointing."

With the emotional loss to Brazil behind them, Team Canada was determined to reward the city for its

130

Dan Galbraith

Dan Galbraith

tremendous support with a bronze medal. "What's important is to leave each mistake behind and carry on," professed Koskie. Facing a strong Argentinean team, Canada gave up the first set, but came on strong and after three exciting matches, team red and white was on the podium accepting the bronze medal. "Standing there on the podium, receiving our medals, watching the Canadian flag go up, I'll never forget it," Koskie confirmed. "It would have been great to hear our anthem, but it was tremendous just to see our flag up there. It was our goal to win a medal and we did."

Koskie lamented that the team didn't play their best volleyball in Winnipeg but credited the crowd for being behind them the whole time, lifting them up. Organizers structured the tournament in a way that encouraged greater spectator excitement. Contests were run as a set of five games, the first four games to 25 (the winning team having to win by two points) and finishing with a rally-point game to 15, as a deciding tiebreaker. Though it isn't the traditional scoring system, awarding points on each play helped maintain the momentum of the game. The new format seemed to win the favour of the athletes as well.

BEACH BALLS

Played on an imported beach in the middle of Winnipeg Stadium, in conditions that often belied the game's name, twelve women's and men's teams gave game-goers a firsthand taste of the international caliber of Beach Volleyball competition. Played on a court that is identical to its indoor cousin, but with only two play-

VOLUNTEERS

ers and the added variables of wind, weather and sand, it is easy to understand why this game is gaining such momentum worldwide. And Canadian teammates Jody Holden and Conrad Leinemann gave the Canadian crowd even more to cheer about.

The east-coast meets west-coast duo came to play. For the love of the game, the thrill of a partisan crowd, and for the glory of a place on the podium, they were ready to lay it all out. Their visualization proved fruitful, landing them on the podium's top step. While the journey and the celebration was Olympic, the gold-medal destination was somewhat precarious. The tournament had no influence on world-rankings, or invitations to the Olympics, but Holden and Leinemann agreed that it was worth the risk of passing over several qualifying tournaments in favour of the shine of the Pan Am Games. "We came to play in front of a crowd like this," Holden explained. "To play and win in Canada is like nothing else. This will ready us for our Olympic dream - we wanted to be put in a high pressure situation like this."

The gold-medal match was intense. The strain, both physical and emotional, showed on both sides of the net. Volleyball, both indoor and outdoor, is as much a mental competition as it is physical. The team that can maintain momentum usually procures the glory. "It's difficult to stay mentally aggressive and focused," Holden clarified. "You've got to dig deep, all the way down to the soles of your feet just to find something to keep you going sometimes." Holden and Leinemann took full advantage of their home court to benefit their

Norm Lourenco

VOLUNTEERS

Dan Galbraith

Norm Lourenco

pursuit of the momentum. Taking their cue from Holden who would encourage their cheers with an upward motion of his arms, the crowd ranted, chanted and raved in their attempt to unnerve the tenacious Brazilians. The strain on the South Americans' faces was telling as serves went long and into the net. The small enclave of boisterous Brazilians who came to bolster their team only fueled the Canadians on to more clamorous levels.

The Canadians took the first game, but Brazil fought back, defeating the home team in the second. Undaunted, the crowd continued in its salute, encouraging the players while dancing and singing with the mascots Pato and Lorita. The rules of the tournament governed that a deciding 12-point match be played in rally style. This ensured that a point was scored on each play and tensions remain taut. "The last game was a pressure-cooker," smiled Lienemann. "You should be in our shorts when we're

VOLUNTEERS

going through that rally," Holden proposed. "This is a dream come true. For us, it's like being at the Olympics because it's on Canadian soil," Holden added. "We were just blown away with emotion."

Holden recounted a previous competition played in Brazil with 8,000 screaming Brazilians. "There were 6,002 people on the court here," said Holden, happy to return the favour. "Our hats go off to the Canadian fans," Lienemann grinned.

VOLUNTEERS

Norm Lourenco

Norm Lourenco

THE RACQUET CLUB

BADMINTON

O R I G I N S Variations of racquet sports have been played for centuries throughout the world. In India, in the mid-19th century, English army officers played a local racquet game called "Poona". They brought the game to England where it caught on quickly. In 1873, the story is told of a group of Poona players at the Duke of Beaufort's estate in Badminton, England, who were forced inside by rain and decided to adapt Poona rules to indoor play. The new variations caught on quickly and eventually evolved into the sport of badminton.

THE PAN AM BADMINTON TOURNAMENT WAS A TRIUMPHANT EVENT FOR CANADA. CANADIAN ATHLETES WALKED AWAY WITH TEN MEDALS, THE MOST OF ANY PAN AM COUNTRY. THE UNITED STATES ALSO TASTED VICTORY WITH A TOTAL OF FIVE MEDALS.

VOLUNTEERS

RACQUETBALL

O R I G I N S Racquetball emerged from a sport known as paddle ball, a game played on a handball court with wooden paddles and a tennis ball. In the 1960s, the sport was revolutionized with the introduction of strong racquets, a rubber ball and the incorporation of specific racquetball rules. The evolution of racquetball continued in 1969, with the formation of the International Racquetball Association, and the name racquetball officially replaced paddle ball and other name variations.

Norm Lourenco

Ken Gigliott

A CHAMPION'S FAREWELL

It was Sherman Greenfeld's Olympics. It was his last hurrah. The prolific 37-year-old Canadian racquetball champion chose the Pan Ams in Winnipeg as his farewell

136

Norm Lourenco

SQUASH

event. "This was the pinnacle of my career," admitted Greenfeld. "To play at home in front of my family and friends at our (racquetball's) Olympics meant everything to me." Greenfeld not only had the privilege of competing on his home turf but he also had the honour of giving the athlete's oath during the Opening Ceremony. "That was a dream come true for me," revealed Greenfeld, adding that the opportunity to represent all the athletes at the Games will be his most enduring memory from the Games.

Greenfeld's storied 20-year career has afforded him many memories, but the two-time world champion and 10-time national champion wanted to end his career on a golden note. But his parting game was for bronze and victory eluded him. "It's time to step aside," acknowledged Greenfeld. "I've had my glory days; now it's someone else's turn." And so goes one of Canada's greatest amateur sports success stories.

O R I G I N S Since the building of the first squash court in Quebec City in the 1800s, the sport of squash has experienced a steady development in Canada. It is estimated that more than 400,000 Canadians play squash recreationally or competitively. Squash Canada, founded in 1914, has more than 400 member clubs.

VOLUNTEERS

Norm Lourenco

TABLE TENNIS

O R I G I N S Early games resembling table tennis were played by the British army in India in the late 1800s. Cigar box tops were used as racquets, corks as balls, and the game was played on a table with a row of books set across the middle instead of a net. When wooden bats and celluloid balls were introduced, the game sparked a craze that swept across England in the late 1800s and into the 1900s. A Ping Pong Association was formed in 1902, but gradually declined due to lack of interest. It was eventually revived as the Table Tennis Association, the name Ping Pong having since become a registered trademark.

VOLUNTEERS

Norm Lourenco

TENNIS

O R I G I N S The earliest forerunners of modern racquet sports were played by striking objects back and forth with the palm of the hand. Racquets, nets and common rules followed. The name "tennis" may have its origin in the French word "tenex" (meaning "hold" or "take heed"), which would have served as a warning of an impending service. The first lawn tennis championships were held in 1877 at Wimbledon, still the site of one of the most prestigious tournaments in the world. Tennis has moved from being a recreational activity for the aristocracy to being a popular athletic event for a wide range of people. Tennis was an official Olympic sport from 1896-1924, then was dropped from the program until 1988.

VICTORY FOR VENEZUELA'S VENTO

Carrying Venezuela's hopes high, the petite and proud Maria Vento put a spectacular finishing touch on her Pan Am dream. Completing a sweep of the top American tennis stars, Vento stormed back from an early deficit to defeat second-seeded Tara Snyder and bring the gold medal home to Venezuela.

After her earlier victories over the U.S.'s third-seeded Lilia Osterloh and top-seeded Alexandra Stevenson in the semi-final, Vento appeared to be spent during the first few games of the final match. Her efforts to lob the ball to Snyder were disastrous, allowing the American to build a 4-0 lead. Then, without warning, Vento regained her composure. Her game turned around completely, and soon it was Snyder who was running for the ball and

139

making errors. The Venezuelan, cheered on by dozens of her fans, never looked back and rode a wave of momentum to the tournament title.

It was the biggest victory in the 25-year-old's professional career, even more special than the gold medal she won last year in the Central American Games. "At the Pan Ams you play totally for your country and it's much more special," stated Vento, the tournament's fifth seed.

VOLUNTEERS

Norm Lourenco

TABLE TALK

The talk around the table - table tennis table, that is - in Winnipeg during the Pan Ams was that the ancient game was going to do the unthinkable: it was going to change. Talk had it that the table tennis world would soon be rocked by the ping-pong equivalent of an earthquake. That is if the International Table Tennis Federation officially approves a change in the size of the ball, which it is expected to do.

The celluloid composite orb will be increased from its traditional 38 millimetres to 40 millimetres. The new ball will slow the game down and make it easier for television cameras to follow, said Marianne Domonkos, women's coach of the Canadian table tennis team since 1988. "It's not that we don't think of ourselves as spectator-friendly," she proposed. "It's just that we want to be more audience friendly."

The "old" ball could travel up to speeds of 100 km/h or more across the 5-by-9-foot table. The change, which has been hotly debated for years in table tennis circles, will not be instituted until after the Sydney Olympics in 2000. The larger ball will not only be heavier - the current one weighs 2.5 grams - but it will meet greater wind resistance and reduced spin. A slower ball makes it easier to follow and tips the game slightly in favour of defensive choppers, who have been losing ground to offensive smashers in the past decade.

VOLUNTEERS

MAKING CONTACT

BOXING

O R I G I N S Ancient Egyptian murals attest to the fact that boxing has existed for more than 6,000 years. Boxing was included in the ancient Olympics. Modern competitive boxing owes much to the Marquis of Queensbury, who in the 1860s drew up a set of rules making boxing a safer sport. The Marquis' rules, which restricted where blows could land, limited rounds to three minutes, and made padded gloves mandatory, are still in place today with some modifications. Amateur bouts are shorter than those in professional boxing, and scoring rules are designed to favour the skillful boxer over the merely powerful boxer.

FIGHT NIGHT AT DUCKWORTH

It is an art in suffering. Some sports are rough by nature, some are rougher by nationality, but boxing is the sole sport that could be classified as purely punishing. And punished most competitors were, by the mighty Cubans who ruled the ring. Cuban amateur boxers have dominated the sport for 20 years, and though the Canadian team fought gallantly, the Cuban powerhouse (with gold contenders in each of the 12 weight classes, nine of them advancing to gold medal matches) proved a tough house to topple.

The sport has its own dark attraction. The arena is sparsely lit and the ring is spotlighted, elevated and open. Enter two fighters glistening and ready to prove

142

Norm Lourenco

Norm Lourenco

143

VOLUNTEERS

Norm Lourenco

their mettle to each other, to the crowd sitting anxiously waiting for the bell to sound, and perhaps most importantly to their country. Their mettle can contribute to the nation's medal count and to its index of accomplishments and glory.

Albeit still related to its professional cousin, amateur boxing's bouts are shorter and the scoring is done electronically. The object nonetheless remains the same: punch and avoid being punched. The bout consists of four, two-minute rounds. Gloves are paneled in white and points are scored for blows landed using the white portion of the mitt. If the referee feels a boxer cannot recover defensively, a standing

VOLUNTEERS

Norm Lourenco

eight-count is enforced. Bouts that last the entire four rounds are evaluated on points awarded.

The seats at the University of Winnipeg's Duckworth Centre were filled for the medal rounds with the hometown crowd cheering wildly for Canada's scrappy gold medal hopefuls as they entered the square ring. The matches proceeded in quick succession starting with the lightest weight class. Dana Laframboise represented Canada in the 60-kg class, with Cuba's Mario Kindelan Mesa taking the gold. Jeremy Molitor lost his gold medal match to a taller and longer Juan Hernandez from Cuba. Hernandez also wears the distinction of four-time world champion and two-time Olympic medallist. Odlaniel Solis kept the Cuban streak alive by defeating Mark Simmons in the 91-kg class. Factoring into their success, the Cuban team trains full-time while many amateur boxers (Canadians included) work full-time and train around their vocational commitments. The Cubans could not be defeated, but the Canadians punched, darted and danced with pride in the fight of their lives.

VOLUNTEERS

FENCING

O R I G I N S The ancient Egyptians may have practiced fencing as a sport; a relief carving in a temple near Luxor depicts a fencing bout in which sword points are covered and face masks worn. Fencing, and more particularly the sword, was one of the earliest weapons of offense and defense. As a weapon of war, its fate was dictated by the progression of technology. With the need for swordplay eventually becoming less, the upper-classes adopted it as a way of settling differences in now famous "duels". The development of fencing as a non-lethal sport began last century and since then has been recognized as a sport of civility and honour. Fencing has been on the Olympic program since the first modern games, and Canada has fielded a team every year since 1928.

Norm Lourenco

SWORD POINT

The Canadian men's sabre team did what no one else could. They stunned the heavily favoured Cuban fencing team to take gold-medal honours. Newcomer Marc-Olivier Hassoun, who did not compete in the individual sabre competition, led the way by first crushing the U.S. team and then the first two Cubans he faced. But then the nineteen-year-old ran into Candido Camejo Maya, Cuba's gold medallist in individual sabre. Maya changed the momentum, bettering Hassoun to give Cuba a slim lead with just two bouts remaining.

Sensing victory, the Cuban athletes and coaches began celebrating on the sidelines. Canada's Michel Boulos was up next; Boulos had lost his previous bout 10-5. "I knew after the bout I lost that I had put the team in a critical situation," Boulos confessed. "I had to give it

Norm Lourenco

Norm Lourenco

Norm Lourenco

my all." That he did, punishing Cuban Buduen Cabaellero by a score of 7-1. Canada had a 40-36 lead with one bout to go.

That left Quebec's 28-year-old Evens Gravel to stave off Jimenez Cabaellero. Twice that week already, a Cuban had snatched possible gold from a Canadian fencer in the dying seconds of a match. But not this time. Gravel, the most experienced fencer on the team, adjusted his game when the Cuban began scoring points on him. The Cubans came within two points of the Canadians at one point in the final bout, but Gravel didn't break and in the end Canada had held for a 45-40 victory over the mighty Cubans. "These are lions!" shouted feisty Canadian coach Henri Sassine, as pandemonium broke out at Maples Complex. Sassine hugged everyone in sight, including several unsuspecting volunteers.

The Cubans had won all nine gold medals up to that point, and a win in sabres would have given them a sweep of fencing events at the Games.

Sabre differs from epee and foil events in that the latter two require that the competitor hits his or her opponent with the sword point to score points. In sabre, the side of the blade is used, and thrusts resemble a cutting action.

VOLUNTEERS

Norm Lourenco

Norm Lourenco

JUDO

O R I G I N S Dr. Jigoro Kano opened the first judo school in Tokyo in 1882 after an exhaustive study of the Japanese martial arts. Kano, a physical educator who had studied at Oxford, eliminated or modified the deadlier moves of other Japanese martial arts to create a physical education program for a broad population. A new combative sport he called judo - "the gentle way" - was born. Emphasizing strength, balance and respect for one's opponent, the sport has now spread throughout the world (today, the International Judo Federation includes 184 national judo federations). When the first world championships were held in 1956, competitors were not divided into weight categories. It was felt that a small, skilled athlete could beat a large, equally skilled opponent. That thinking changed over the years. There are currently seven weight classes for men and women.

VOLUNTEERS

Don Gaudette

KARATE

ORIGINS The origins of a number of martial arts are said to have come from the legendary Bodhidharma, a Buddhist monk who came from India and settled in China. His teachings later became the basis for the majority of Chinese martial arts. Little more is known about the roots of karate until it appeared on the Japanese island of Okinawa. Because weapons bans were imposed on Okinawans at various points in their history, residents developed various forms of karate. Karate, which means "empty hand", began to spread earlier this century when public demonstrations of karate in Japan captured the imagination of people such as Japanese Crown-Prince Hirohito and Dr. Kano, the founder of judo.

VOLUNTEERS

TAE KWON DO

O R I G I N S The Korean martial art of tae kwon do has roots dating back more than 2,000 years. Murals painted during the Koguro dynasty of ancient Korea depict two men performing an activity that looks like tae kwon do. "Tae" means jumping and kicking; "kwon" means striking and blocking with the hand, and "do" means "the way." The sport places more emphasis on kicks than it does on blows with the hands. Like other martial arts, it also emphasizes ethics and tradition.

U N F O R G E T T A B L E

The second to last day of competition at the 1999 Pan American Games is a day that Team Canada's Roxanne Forget will always remember. It was the day that Quebec's petite Forget came out of nowhere to win Pan Am gold in tae kwon do. Forget beat American Kay Poe in an unforgettable match that had the packed crowd at the Winnipeg Convention Centre screaming all the way to the victorious end. Down by one point after the first round and tied after two, Forget came on strong in the third frame to win by four points and claim Team Canada's only gold in Winnipeg's tae kwon do competition. "This is my best performance ever, the best crowd ever," announced Forget enthusiastically.

Norm Lourenco

152

Dan Galbraith

MODERN PENTATHLON

O R I G I N S The sport of modern pentathlon simulates the trials of a military courier charged with delivering a message by horseback through hostile territory. After he loses his horse, the messenger defends himself with pistol and sword, swims a river and runs across the countryside to accomplish his mission. Thus, the sport's five events are shooting, fencing, swimming, riding and running. Baron Pierre de Coubertin, who is considered to be the founder of the modern Olympics, asked that modern pentathlon be included in the 1912 Games in Stockholm. De Coubertin wanted to revive the spirit of the pentathlon of the ancient Greeks. The ancient pentathlete wrestled, ran the length of the stadium, jumped and threw the spear and the discus. Competitors with a military background have dominated the modern pentathlon.

VOLUNTEERS

SKILL, SPEED & STAMINA

Arguably, the modern pentathlon is the ultimate test for an athlete. This unique one-day event requires athletes to complete five sports - air pistol shooting, fencing, swimming (200 metres), horse jumping and running (3,000 metres) - all in a span of less than twelve hours. Athletes must combine skill, speed, stamina and mental focus. From a relaxed and focused state in the fencing and shooting events, athletes must then go all out in the swim. Complete cooperation with a horse is followed by running a strategic race to determine the event winner.

An athlete's placing in each of the first four events is converted into points. Competitors are then staggered according to point totals to start the 3,000 metre run. As such, this "chase-race" format determines the overall event winner to be the one to cross the finish line first.

Dan Galbraith

Norm Lourenco

Norm Lourenco

WRESTLING

O R I G I N S Techniques used in modern wrestling go back to the ancient civilizations of China, Egypt and Greece. Wrestling was included as early as 704 B.C. as one of the events in the ancient Greek Olympics. The Romans, who conquered the Greek empire, developed the Greco-Roman style by eliminating the use of the legs. Being a wrestler in ancient times was not necessarily a safe profession, as few of the modern rules that restrict the risk of injury were in place.

155

Norm Lourenco

WEATHERING THE STORM

If only Wayne Weathers could light a fire under his Winnipeg Blue Bomber teammates the way he did with his freestyle wrestling squad. Showing the intensity of a linebacker after a quarterback, Weathers wasted almost no time getting things done in his bronze-medal bout - pinning Venezuela's Jose Marin in just 25 seconds. In that short time, the 26-year-old Canadian Football League player erased any doubt as to why he's considered Canada's top freestyle grappler in his heavy-weight class. He completely outworked the Venezuelan before putting his opponent's shoulders to the mat for the fall.

"I wanted to get something I could send home to my mom, and that's what I did," said the 6-foot-4 Weathers after the fight. His short-order performance was the most high-profile victory in the Oshawa native's 15-year wrestling career, setting the stage for his run at an Olympic berth.

In all, seven of Canada's eight freestylists joined the medal parade. Canada's solid third-place showing in freestyle, a monumental improvement after getting just one bronze in Greco-Roman competition, came with a sharp reversal in the top two spots. After Cuba's domination of Greco-Roman, the U.S. controlled freestyle.

But the real winner may have been amateur wrestling in Manitoba, the only province that doesn't include the sport at the high school level. Competition director Nat Brigante said that could soon change, with talks under way now to include wrestling as a demonstration school sport in years ahead.

VOLUNTEERS

Dan Galbraith

ROLLER SPORTS

O R I G I N S The origin of roller skating goes back to 17th century Holland, where a Dutchman, reluctant to put away his ice skates after the canals thawed, fastened wooden spools to his shoes and took up "ground skating." A Belgian inventor and instrument maker named Joseph Merlin is credited with making the first patented roller skate in 1760. The early skates had a single row of wheels in a straight line, and truly were the forerunner of today's inline skates. Technological improvements gradually made roller skates more stable and more manoeuverable, in turn helping roller skating develop as a recreational activity and a competitive sport. Until recently, most competitors used skates with two sets of side-by-side wheels. In recent years, however, the popularity of inline skates has surged, and they are used almost exclusively in speed skating and hockey events. Inlines are also becoming the skate of choice for some competitors in the artistic discipline.

F O O L ' S   G O L D

So much to be positive about; then ironically positive it was and all that was good came crashing down. The euphoria surrounding the men's inline roller hockey team's gold medal victory was short-lived. The underdog Canadians played a game that will not soon be forgotten by those who witnessed it. The Canadian men outscored the favoured Americans by one goal for the win, the gold, and for their first-ever victory over the U.S. in international competition. The victory was great cause for celebration. Even on wheels, any hockey game between

Canada and the United States ignites a nationalist fervor.

On a terribly hot and humid night, in a packed arena, fans gulped down ice cold water as fast as they could: anything to try to keep cool at the "ol' hockey arena." The Canadians came out flying and played an inspired game. The suspense was unbearable at times as the scoreboard kept track of the goal for goal game.

The game was sold out days in advance. Ticket scalpers were buzzing around the front doors of the rink touting the showdown between the hockey powers for gold. The media piled into the sweat box to catch what was likely going to be the talk of the Games. Nothing could have been closer to the truth.

The rules of inline hockey are slightly different than ice hockey. There are only nine floor players and one goaltender on each team - only four skaters per side on the floor at once. There is no checking and no fighting. Each game is played in two 20-minute periods, with a five minute intermission between them. An inline hockey game has no "icing" or "offside" infractions. Some ice hockey fans may not understand the appeal of the game. However, after watching the round robin match between Canada and the U.S., new-found fans were abound.

Dan Galbraith

Throughout the final match the crowd was on the edge of its seat. They roared, they ooed, they cheered and when the 'last minute of play' was announced with a 7-6 lead for Canada nearly sealed, the crowd went crazy. To hockey fans, the inline team brought Canada's game home. The athletes wore their shiny gold medals with pride; they fought hard for the deserved win. No one could have predicted the events that were about to unfold.

Before the ensuing celebrations had a chance to subside there was news that the gold was to be returned. The United States were to be the champions. Steve Vezina, the 23-year-old Canadian goaltender, had been caught cheating. He tested positive for stimulants and massive amounts of anabolic steroids. Vezina acknowledged that he had

Jeff De Booy

taken the cold remedy Sudafed - used by a number of professional athletes as a game-day performance enhancer - during the Games. He also admitted to taking Nandrolone, capsules which he had purchased at a pharmacy to combat weight loss attributed to his busy roller hockey schedule.

There was outrage in Winnipeg when news hit that the players would be stripped of their medals. Vezina was already back in his hometown, near Montreal, Quebec. It took several days before he would address the public and his teammates. As his teammates waited patiently for his response, their allegiance to their goalie started to wane. Reality started to sink in. Anger began to build. Kevin Kerr, a North Bay, Ontario native, scored the winning goal in the emotional victory match. His reaction epitomized the nation's collective response: "He ruined the chance of a lifetime for nine guys." Kerr went on to assert that, "I know I, along with the others, were clean. We did it the way we were supposed to. There are guys on this team that will never have an opportunity to represent their country again."

Scott Burfoot, of Winnipeg, was stunned after he heard the devastating news. "This is one of the toughest things I've ever had to do in my life," he said in reference to returning the medal. "I wore it around my neck for two days. I kissed it. It was the greatest feeling winning in front of our home fans, and now it's gone."

Winnipeg's Jeff Leiter was shocked by the news as well. "The doping regulations were explained to us. The Canadian Olympic Association warned us about banned substances on numerous occasions, long before we got here. We were given a booklet that was about a half-inch thick when we arrived for the Games, and the opportunity to report on anything taken."

When Vezina finally appeared at a news conference at a Golf and Country Club outside Montreal he apologized to his teammates but went on to claim that he didn't do anything wrong. "I'm a professional athlete and an ice hockey player first and these substances are tolerated." Vezina went on to say, "Other professionals take them and they're heroes; I take a little bit to get me ready for ice hockey and it seems it would be less bad if I robbed a bank." His teammates had heard more than enough. Doctor Andrew Pipe, Canada's leading dope crusader contradicted Vezina's confession: "This is probably the largest level I have ever seen reported."

And so it was that the United States inline hockey team owned the gold, Argentina received the silver and Brazil moved up into the medals in the bronze position. Leiter appeared on national television with a message for

Norm Lourenco

VOLUNTEERS

Norm Lourenco

his mates. "Still be proud of what we've done and as tough as it is I think we accomplished a lot."

No one can take away the excitement of that game, the victory or the pride that swept through the Max Bell arena that night. On that hot summer's night in Winnipeg, the Canadian men's inline hockey team brought Canada's game back home, even if only for a moment.

HELL ON WHEELS

From Cyndy Klassen's perspective, the 1999 Pan Ams stand as a personal best performance for her, but the Games also leaked out Roller Speed skating's unsavoury little secret. The 19-year-old from Winnipeg sat in third place in the women's sprints after the first of three races at the outdoor track at Grant Park. Klassen beat her own personal best time by a full second, a result that surprised even her. "It was just incredible," Klassen beamed. "I went to the Worlds last year and I didn't have a chance against other racers but here in Winnipeg I actually beat some of them."

Klassen is convinced that the hometown crowd made her wheels roll a little faster. "It's so comforting knowing I'm racing on home turf. My family and friends were there to cheer me on. The adrenaline really got me moving."

It was a magical moment for Klassen to compete in the Pan Am Games and she revealed that it was a milestone in her career. However, Klassen experienced first-hand Roller Speed skating's downfall. Nothing she wasn't

161

VOLUNTEERS

Norm Lourenco

ONE OF THE COOLEST SOUVENIRS AT THE GAMES WERE THE BROKEN
IN-LINE HOCKEY TILES AT U OF M'S MAX BELL ARENA.

aware of, but this time it hit too close to home. It started when two male skaters were disqualified when they began fist fighting during a race. Then the women's half-marathon was marred when the champion American skater was pulled from behind by a Chilean skater just before she was about to launch her sprint to the finish line. And then Klassen's dream of winning bronze was shattered when an Argentinean skater reached out during the 500-metre race and forcefully pulled her back, and out of contention for a medal. "That's why this sport can't get into the Olympics," declared Klassen. "There's a big debate as to whether there should have been more race officials during the Games but competitors know that when you race against some of the other countries, prepare for a shoving match."

VOLUNTEERS

Blocking and elbowing are against the rules during Roller Speed races and competitors can be penalized or even disqualified, if caught. But rough play continues to occur and that may be one reason why the Olympic Committee won't look at the sport as one that could be included in future Olympic Games. "I realize that the pushing and shoving aren't in the spirit of competition. We as competitors must clean up the sport before we'll ever be allowed to compete in the Olympics," Klassen professed. "But that's for later; for now I'm proud of my accomplishments and I'm proud to say I'm from Manitoba."

Norm Lourenco

Norm Lourenco

VOLUNTEERS

BODY, MIND & SPIRIT

ARTISTIC &
RHYTHMIC GYMNASTICS

O R I G I N S The word "gymnastics" comes from the ancient Greeks, who used the word in a more generic sense to refer to physical activity. The Romans adopted Greek ideas of physical culture, and incorporated gymnastics into military training. They performed an early version of today's vault by building wooden dummy horses upon which to practice mounting and dismounting. In the last two centuries, the sport has become formalized with the specific types of apparatus and scoring procedures used today.

Dan Galbraith

CHANGING OF THE GUARD

In a demonstration of pure tenacity, strength and courage the Canadian women's gymnastics team achieved what their predecessors could not since 1979 in San Juan.

It had been twenty years since Canada had won the team gold in Artistic Gymnastics. They wrested the gold from the reigning world champion American squad and in the process captured the hearts of the fans. Competing in vault, uneven bars, balance beam and the popular floor routine the team put up top scores in each event, surprising even themselves just a little.

"We were concentrating completely on team," team captain Yvonne Tousek beamed. "We didn't go in there thinking where we wanted to place. We just had to do the best we could and the rest would take care of itself." With each routine the team gained confidence and enthusiasm. Talent took care of the rest. Noticeably overwhelmed at the girls' spectacular performance, their coach thanked the spectators and press for their patronage, an impromptu public relations effort on behalf of the sport. "I think the international community is going to look at us in a different way now; publicity for gymnastics is very much needed in Canada," she volunteered.

"We did the best job we could," asserted Tousek, the veteran of the team at 19 years old. "To make Canada proud was an amazing feeling." Word spread quickly about the team's success and with four members with individual competitions to come, attendance for gym-

Dan Galbraith

166

Dan Galbraith

nastic events more than doubled in the days that followed. They were not disappoint-
ed. After a successful showing at the apparatus finals, Tousek earned gold medals for
her routines on the floor and the uneven bars. Lise Leveille took gold in the beam routine and teammates Julie Beaulieu and Michelle Conway each accepted silver for the
uneven bars and floor routine respectively.

Although Tousek had her moment to shine, it was Conway who surprised every-

• Stanley Zapart • Dominique Zapart • Christina Dolinski • Candice BrigdenKontzie • Roxanne Somorjai • Stephen Doolan • Chandra Jackson • David Holt • Scott Schinkel • Louise Cooke • Ralph Oliver • Alan Wall • Krista Munro • Leslie Manness • Leslie Manness • Maureen Watson • Ana Hernandez • Krystal Bartkiewicz • Jackie Cole • Kathryn Wolos • Rose Thomas • Beverley Brown • Benjamin Johnson • Gordon Ayotte • Peter Waldie • Michael McMurray • Ron Ottawa • Eliude Cavalcante • Sandy James Watts • Richard Wolfson • Kimberley McCallumGrier • Kimberley McCallum • SaraJane Schmidt • Matthew Yathon • Denyse Johnson • Julie Blais • Laurie Grzenda • Jennifer Chan • Louise Evans • Alex Leligdowicz • Karen Appel • Jennifer Trachtenberg • Jennifer Janzen • Lisa Whalen • Cara Hutchison • Debra Evaniuk • Goldie Dhaliwal • Bianca Carriere • Geoffrey Palmer • Ken Nolin • Alysa Poulin • Leigh Adams • Krista Goodridge • Heather Foubert • Serena Puranen • Marissa Szajcz • Linda MacDiarmid • treu • Frank Arsenault • Dustin Whyte • Ryan Brite • Lindsay Wawryko • Fay Stefanec • Carla Wenger • Adams Hayward • Patricia Cassie • Susan Beharnell • Valerie Moore • Eric Sagenes • Judy Hudey • Aliza Andrews • Isobel Wheeler • Cindy Radford • Sonia Matwyczuk • Sonia Matwyczuk • Mark Freed • Gloria McBurney • Gloria McBurney • Robin ParkesIlchuk • Cathy Brown • Lisanne Cindric • Macgregor Stephens • Bob Chochinov • Richard Graydon • Cheryl Costen • Karen Heinrichs • Alison Elliott • letcalfe • Carol Hennessy • Judy Sigler • Donna Talbot • Lori Versavel • Monique Rear • April Keedian • Sandra Klinck • Thomas Rossi • Yvonne VernausScott • Lucy Glaw • Terry Baxter • Paul Winslow • Robert Town • Robert Town • Ron Snider • Edward Schwark • James Ross • Bill Osachuk • Robert Norris • Gerald McArthur • Lawrence Martin • Jim Kushnowski • Morris Kagan • Al Jelliff • Cal Hunter • Dennis Handford • Pat Einarson • Larry Dreger • Glenn Dodd • Brent Dixon • Dennis Deley • Larry Crane lements • Jack Carmichael • Peter Campbell • Peter Campbell • Don Cameron • Bill Bracegirdle • Bill Bracegirdle • Bill Bracegirdle • Blaine Bartley • Nancy Krueger • Ashley Skrabek • Donna Smith • Judith Daniels • Doreen Goring • Crystle Kozoroski • Maureen Fryza • Julius Rucki • ElÉonore Philibert • Ilana Bleichert • David Kives • Joan Alleyne • Shirley Hampton • Denise Reitsma • Jackie Derkson • Richard Pawlosky • Sarah Conci • Judy Todd • Elaine Taylor • Blaine Cleghorn • William Young • Alexander

VOLUNTEERS

one with her performance in the overall individual competition. Again ending a drought that dated back to 1979, Conway was the first Canadian to earn a medal standing in that event in 20 years. "Michelle has the ability to really project and grab an audience," voiced her coach. "She's a good tumbler, but so often tumblers don't know how to grab a crowd."

"Louder is always better," Conway said about the crowd. "It helps me with my energy breathing. Having everyone behind me just gives me a little bit more. Especially being at home," Conway smiled.

Dan Galbraith

Dan Galbraith

VOLUNTEERS

Dan Galbraith

VOLUNTEERS

TRIATHLON

O R I G I N S Although the three sports that make up triathlon have each been around for many years, their combination into a single sport is a relatively new phenomenon. The first known events took place in San Diego's Mission Bay in 1974, when they were organized on summer evenings after work as a light-hearted break from traditional run training. A U.S. Naval officer attended one of these events and brought the triathlon concept to Hawaii. The result was the first "Iron Man" in 1978, consisting of a 3.8 kilometre swim, a 180 km cycle and a 42 km run. In 1989 the International Triathlon Union (ITU) was formed at the inaugural world championships in Avignon, France. Today, the ITU includes over 80 countries. Triathlon first appeared on the Pan American Games program in 1995 and makes its Olympic debut at the 2000 games in Sydney.

Norm Lourenco

Norm Lourenco

TRIATHLETE TAKES FLIGHT

With the Games only several days old, Sharon Donnelly graciously accepted the title
of "Golden Girl" after winning the women's triathlon. Such status was certainly attrib-
utable to her gold-medal victory in the grueling event, but it was the subsequent meeting of Golden Boy that solidified it.

A second-time Pan Am event, the triathlon included a 1.5-kilometre swim, a 40-
km bike race and finished with a 10-km run. Donnelly attacked each as if there was
nothing to lose but the gold medal. That in fact was the case. With four previous top-
10 finishes in four World Cup races Donnelly had already earned her spot on Team
Canada's entry at the 2000 Sydney Olympics, the first time the triathlon will be included as an Olympic medal event. Supported by 1,500 stalwart fans who braved the 32
degree Celsius heat and humidity to cheer on the resolute athletes, Donnelly com-

Norm Lourenco

VOLUNTEERS

mended them all on their indomitable spirit. "This is the biggest and the most committed event, from a city perspective, that I've ever been to," she shouted.

Donnelly, a military reservist, had her triumphant performance complemented with a symbolic Armed Forces helicopter flight over the City of Winnipeg, an indulgence of the 408 Tactical Helicopter Squadron. The unit was intent on taking one of the military's own over the city's Golden Boy, perched high atop the province's Legislative Building. The Golden Boy is a 4-metre-tall statue representing the spirit of enterprise and eternal youth. Sculpted and cast in France, the icon crowned the Legislature when it opened in 1920.

"I'm just one of many golden girls," Donnelly offered humbly among a throng of reporters and endearing fans anxious to greet Canada's "ironwoman" upon her return. Donnelly was overwhelmed by her newly acquired celebrity. The Games' first Golden Girl was suddenly monopolized by autograph seekers curious to get a glimpse of the gold medal dangling proudly around her neck. In effect, Sharon Donnelly was still airborne.

Norm Lourenco

VOLUNTEERS

Norm Lourenco

WEIGHTLIFTING

O R I G I N S Throughout history, people have competed against each other in tests of strength. During the 1800s, professional strongmen showed off feats of strength in European music halls and circuses. French Canadian Louis Cyr was the strongest of the professional strongman in the late 1800s and early 1900s. Competitive weightlifting grew out of these shows as well as out of a network of athletic clubs that surfaced around the same time. Competitions became regularized after 1920 with the formation of the International Weightlifting Federation. Before that, competitions were held using a number of lifts, many of them one-handed. This was the first time women's weightlifting has been on the Pan American Games program.

173

At the Centennial Concert Hall, a supportive crowd cheered "arriba! arriba!" (up! up!) as Cuba's Hidalberto Aranda took hold of a 205.5 kg barbell. Seconds later, the judges unanimously signaled a good lift and Aranda, who weighs 76.55 kg, had a world weightlifting record in the under 77 kg class. Dropping the barbell, Aranda leaped high above bar and bells in triumph.

CLOSE TO 1,000 RAUCOUS WINNIPEGGERS RAISED THE ROOF OF THE CENTENNIAL CONCERT HALL WITH CHEERS AND SHOUTS OF ENCOURAGEMENT AT THE MERE ANNOUNCING OF THE TWO CANADIAN ATHLETES' NAMES WHO WERE DUELING IT OUT IN THE 75-KILOGRAMS WEIGHTLIFTING COMPETITION. IN THE END IT COULD NOT HAVE BEEN ANY CLOSER FOR BRONZE, BUT IT COULD NOT BE SHARED EITHER. DESPITE LIFTING THE SAME WEIGHT, CANADA'S TWO WOMEN WEIGHTLIFTERS CAME AWAY WITH ONLY ONE BRONZE. IT WENT TO 18-YEAR-OLD JEAN LASSEN OF WHITEHORSE, THE YOUNGEST AMONG ALL WEIGHTLIFTING COMPETITORS AT THE GAMES. WINNIPEG'S LOCAL FAVOURITE, 34-YEAR-OLD THERESA BRICK, PLACED FOURTH. BOTH ATHLETES LIFTED THE SAME WEIGHT - 210 KG - BUT BECAUSE LASSEN IS LIGHTER IN WEIGHT HERSELF, SHE SNATCHED THE BRONZE. WANDA RIJO, 20, OF THE DOMINICAN REPUBLIC, TOOK GOLD WITH A LIFT OF 220 KG.

Norm Lourenco

VOLUNTEERS

Norm Lourenco

VOLUNTEERS

"If there is one true legacy of the Games - past the new facilities and fresh coats of paint, beyond the financial boon and the gallons of newspaper ink - it is that we have learned who we are and what we believe in."

LINDOR REYNOLDS

LEGACY

A FAREWELL TO THE AMERICAS

It was a tough act to follow. The Opening Ceremony had been an undeniable success. So was the Closing Ceremony, chiefly because it did not even try to compete with what was the opening night. Trading the spectacularly emotional, lump-in-your-throat reception for a get-up-and-dance soiree, Winnipeg's last hurrah, full of Latin American flavour, suggested that the torch had assuredly been passed to Santo Domingo, the host of the XIV Pan American Games.

The evening began traditionally, with the introduction of government and Pan American Games officials. The focus soon shifted to the heart and soul of the Games. It

Boris Minkevich

was a passionate moment, as thousands of seated Games volunteers, joined by thousands of appreciative others, saluted their own - a stream of volunteers paraded into the stadium waving in acceptance to the bestowal of admiration. Lead by Pato and Lorita, the assemblage represented only a fraction of the entire army of volunteers that made the Games a success. From the sea of salmon-shirted volunteers who filled every conceivable role as required, to the medical volunteers, security attaches, the police, the Red

VOLUNTEERS

Cross, the military personnel, the Salvation Army, and finally the RCMP who marched majestically in time, it was a heartfelt moment at Winnipeg Stadium.

The countdown had begun. Only seconds until airtime. The anticipation was tangible throughout the stands. Back from opening night, in flew the geese, creating a corridor for the athletes' final entrance. In they danced, nations intermingled, in a symbolic gesture of the friendships that the Games fostered. Showered with bouquets of colourful streamers, images from the Open Ceremony lit up Panasonic's Astrovision screen. The crowd cheered and cheered. The athletes lapped it up, waving, blowing kisses, prancing and shuffling for all those who came to say good-bye. Many carried signs thanking the people of Winnipeg for their hospitality.

Don MacKenzie, President and CEO of the Pan American Games Society, delivered the introductory speech, a tribute to the accomplishments of the athletes, officials, volunteers and "the memories that would last a lifetime." MacKenzie concluded prophetically: "The Pan Am flame will be extinguished this evening, but the spirit of the Games will endure in our memories and in the many legacies that will prosper in our communities." Followed by what may have been the most stirring of the addresses, Winnipeg Mayor Glen Murray assured Winnipeggers of what they already knew. "You have defined what athleticism and citizenship are all about. I am humbled to be your Mayor. Winnipeg is, and always will be, the heart of this great country and a home town to all the Americas." He ended his oration with a volley of multilingual thank-yous and a tribute to the diversity that defines the Pan American identity.

In recognition of the next generation of athletes and volunteers, a children's ensemble took to the stadium floor with their production "The Children of the World". Led by spunky 11-year-old Katherine Lee Raymond and accompanied by Nicole Bremault and the celebrated Fred Penner, hundreds of children flooded the field in waves of bright colours and whimsical ribbons.

Manitoba Premier Gary Filmon punctuated their message in the address that followed with his own inspiring words. "Take every opportunity to celebrate the good things in life. Follow your dreams. Here in the heart of Canada ... you've proven once again that Manitobans can do anything and do it world class." Prime Minister Jean Chretien was next to approach the podium, reiterating an athlete salute and the praise

Boris Minkevich

179

VOLUNTEERS

Norm Lourenco

Boris Minkevich

for the people of Winnipeg and Manitoba for making the Pan Am memories possible. "To each and every athlete I want to thank you for allowing us the privilege of watching your dreams come true." Citing the true legacy of the Games, the Prime Minister reminded all to remember the "friendships that were forged on the playing fields." To the city he offered these words of commendation: "All of Canada is proud of you."

Then it was time for Mario Vazquez Rana, President of the Pan American Sports Organization, to put his stamp of approval on the Games. Reminiscent of the Opening Ceremony, Rana's official remarks were again interrupted by the wave - a harmonious crowd body-cheer - that completely encircled the stadium three to four times consecutively. Initiated by the athletes, Rana found it hard to refrain from smiling. He even applauded the crowd's interruption. Upon continuing, his lengthy recitation was redeemed by complimenting Winnipeg for capping the millennium with "the best Games of our history."

A steady rain showered down. While many athletes left their unsheltered seats to seek refuge, the stalwart volunteers once more displayed their dedication by riding it out in their seats, enjoying the show before them. The flags were lowered and the mayor of Santo Domingo was presented with the Pan American Games flag from Mayor Murray. Renowned vocalists Tracy Dahl and Henriette Schellenberg, accompanied by the Pan

Boris Minkevich

VOLUNTEERS

"I have a four-year-old son, and I want him to know that I was involved in the Pan Am Games ... somethir for him to be proud of when he's old enough I want him to have all my pins." *Chris Prince, Securi*

Am Choir, together sang the "Ode to the Athletes". The two women looked magnificent in their shimmering white, sequined gowns. Their performance instantaneously enveloped the stadium, holding the audience captive in quiet wonder. Hundreds of white-robed choir members filed onto the playing field from the four corners surrounding center stage. With one fluid, dramatic movement, multiple bouquets of colourful streamers were hoisted into the air; the choir turned and bowed to the athletes who in turn stood to accept the accolades.

The official end of the 1999 Pan Am Games was near. The Dominican Republic's flag was raised bringing the crowd back to its feet. The Dominican national anthem was played. The Pan Am cauldron faded to black. It was now history, except for the ensuing celebration. The show was now in the hands of the performers. An eruption of fireworks and Latin music welcomed throngs of colourful dancers framed by the uniformity of the choir, which danced around the perimeter of the field. The audience was encouraged to join the party by releasing the balloons provided upon entering the stadium. The entire field was a wash of colour. Trucks transporting steel drum bands crawled onto the field and a seemingly never-ending cast of wonderfully costumed dancers spilled in from each entrance. Anticipation escalated as the crowd caught the contagious fever of the dancers. If it was still raining, no one cared. It was time to embrace the celebration. The athletes poured out onto the field to join in the festivities. The spectators danced and clapped in the stands.

A quartet of Dominican athletes found their "mambo" partner among the evening's Honourary Guests. The mayor of Santo Domingo jigged delightfully with them, to the thunderous applause of the endearing crowd. The stadium floor was alive again.

In keeping with the two-hour schedule of the Ceremony, the party was forced to peak prematurely. A conspicuous crowd circled the end-zone stage where a motif of musical instruments waited to be electrified. The stadium went dark. The Astrovision screen set the stage for Winnipeg's final act. Scenes from Canada's pop past appeared: a prairie group of four young men, dressed in matching mod-suits, with the distinction of quietly changing the face of rock music. By introduction, "a blue-collar band in a blue-collar town, making blue-collar music for the world," it was what Winnipeg had all been waiting for, the reunification of the Guess Who. Band leader and lead vocalist

Boris Minkevich

181

VOLUNTEERS

Burton Cummings addressed the nostalgic gathering. "The four of us owe everything we have to this city. This is a very emotional night for us." A condensed four-song twenty-minute performance closed with what every Guess Who fan was longing for - their signature tune, "American Woman". Winnipeg Stadium was shaking. Youngsters took their cues from their parents, who proudly sang along to the lyrics as if they were their own. The last note resonated out from the amplifiers; the crowd's thrill was deafening. Perhaps another historic moment. The scream of fireworks that hurled high above the stadium served as the encore. The rain had ended. The sky exploded in lights with an impressive display of colour and motion. And with one last fulminating boom the Games were over. All was dark.

Norm Lourenco

182

VOLUNTEERS

Dan Galbraith

HOME SWEET HOME

Winnipeg proved to provide the home-town advantage for Canadian athletes. For only the second time in history, Canadians placed second overall in medals won at the Pan Am Games. The first time was in Winnipeg in 1967. "This will go down as one of the finest Pan Am teams of this century," exclaimed Alex Carre, chef de mission of the Canadian delegation.

The Canadian team left Winnipeg with a number of firsts as well. The 186 medals won is the highest number of medals ever won by Canadians at a Pan Am Games. The 59 gold-medal performances also exceeded all previous top finish totals. "These Games have provided us with some magic moments we'll all remember for some time," said Carre. "Our compliments go out to the organizing committee and the people of Winnipeg. They have set a standard of excellence which will be difficult to duplicate."

THE ULTIMATE SOUVENIR More than pins or T-shirts, the specially crafted 2,300 gold, silver and bronze medals were the real souvenirs of the Pan Am Games. The medals were designed by Pan Am Games Society artists and crafted in Montreal by Henry Birks and Sons, who also fashioned the medals for the 1967 Games in Winnipeg.

The medals display the Games logo on one side with the text "Pan American Games" in English, French and Spanish, while the other side displays a sculpture which adorns the statued corners of the base of the dome of Manitoba's Legislative Building. The sculpture depicts art, culture and heritage. At 70 millimetres in diameter and five millimetres thick, they embody a physical heft to match their symbolic weight.

Dan Galbraith

VOLUNTEERS

Dan Galbraith

WITH GLOWING HEARTS LINDOR REYNOLDS, WINNIPEG FREE PRESS

As Canadians, we tend to define ourselves by what we are not. We are not American. We are not slick or hostile or made mad by crowds pressing against us on narrow sidewalks every working day. We are not controversial or confrontational. We don't make scenes or call attention to ourselves.

The adjective we use to describe our ideal behaviour is "polite." And then the Pan Am Games come to town and thousands of us are sporting maple leafs, waving flags and sniffling when we hear our national anthem played. We are loud, enthusiastic, and very proud. We have been given permission - no, we have been strongly encouraged - to wear our patriotism on our sleeves. This is the gift the Pan Am Games gave to the country. It's the gift Winnipeg gave to itself.

If there is one true legacy of the Games - past the new facilities and fresh coats of paint, beyond the financial boon and the gallons of newspaper ink - it is that we have learned who we are and what we believe in. For 17 days, we opened our hearts to our athletes and cheered them on in unimaginable contests of strength, power and finesse.

VOLUNTEERS

"You want to do something for the community. A group of us from the Shriners, we have a motorcycle unit, and we're helping the media doing courier service with film. I enjoy riding my motorcycle and I'm getting to help the Games in a small way at the same time." *Larry Cra*

The Games taught us what it means to be Canadian. It taught our visitors who we actually are. "I'm leaving thinking about how embraced I was by this city," said Joe Jaffie, a paralegal from Long Island, N.Y., who came to volunteer. "I have been welcomed everywhere I went. This is a special place."

Everyone involved has a special Pan Am moment, a defining image that they will revisit with fondness and nostalgia. For many, it was the sight of Tanya Dubnicoff carrying our flag into the stadium at the Opening Ceremony, leading a sea of our red-and-white clad athletes into sight. "This was a once-in-a-lifetime opportunity," said teacher Kelli Madziuk, who appeared in the ceremonies. "It's a huge deal to me."

It was the Mounties walking onto the field with their huge flag, the national anthem playing and people you had never met before coming up and hugging you because you were wearing a Canadian lapel pin and they were grateful to be here. It's something true and pure that you want your children to feel so they will understand who they are and what it means to be Canadian.

It is B.C.'s Leah Pells missing gold in the women's 1,500 metres by the merest fraction of a second, taking silver in a thrilling contest finally decided by a photo finish. Or Winnipeg's own Kelly Stefanyshyn earning gold in the 100-metre backstroke. Or beach volleyball players Conrad Leinemann and Jody Holden winning gold in a sport we didn't know we cared about until the final match was played. We cheered them all. And we cheered the other nations too, waving the flags of Surinam, the Netherlands Antilles, Belize ... countries we might not have been able to find on a map before the Games.

You define yourself by your actions and your heart. The Pan Am Games have allowed us that chance. The people of Winnipeg shone as a city and, by reflection, as a country. It's only a pity these Games don't happen more often.

21ST CENTURY PAN AMS

The Pan Am Games will survive and flourish only if they become the Olympic qualifying event for every sport involved maintains Mario Vazquez Rana, the President of the Pan American Sports Organization (PASO). Rana's comments were made at a news conference held in Winnipeg during the Games.

Rana explained that both the increase in competition for the athletes' time and the draw of world championship events that offer prize money are squeezing the Pan Am Games and forcing athletes to choose between money and medals. "It is urgent to change the Pan Am Games into the qualifying games for the Olympics," he professed.

Don Gaudette

TEERS

"We have convinced 15 national sports federations to come on board. When we get all 28 to agree, the status of the Pan Am Games will be significantly different. An athlete will not ignore the Pan Am Games if they are a step toward Olympic prestige and the endorsements that follow. "Rana hopes to reach an agreement with all the sports federations and Olympic committees within the Pan American countries before the next Pan Am Games set for Santo Domingo, Dominican Republic, in 2003. Rana feels that bringing all the best Pan American athletes to the Games will enable PASO to request more money from the host city; the right to host the Games will cost committees $2 million, up from the current $1 million that Winnipeg was required to remunerate.

PAN AMERICAN WOMEN

Since the 1995 Pan Am Games in Argentina, women's participation in the Games has skyrocketed. In Mar Del Plata, only 29 women's teams were entered, compared with 68 men's teams. In 1999, 47 women's teams competed, while the men's contingent had only grown by one team - the roller hockey event.

On any given day at the 1999 Pan Am Games, spectators were able to watch women competing in brawny, brawling sports such as water polo, team handball and basketball. But fans also enjoyed more stereotypically feminine pursuits such as synchronized swimming and rhythmic gymnastics. Most importantly, the fans watched in droves.

Keith Levit

The women's softball tournament attracted more fans than the men's tournament and crowds for women's water polo were equal to those watching the men compete. Women's volleyball, basketball and team handball also had big draws. Softball made its Olympic debut to great fanfare in Atlanta and at the 2000 Games in Sydney, women will compete, along with the men, in water polo for the first time. Women's soccer made its debut in Winnipeg. Large, boisterous crowds were a testament to the sport's recent spike in popularity.

AND THAT'S THE NEWS

The Pan Am Games were a made-in-Canada event with big-name sponsors and big-time backing from media. Not only did Canadian broadcasters set up shop for the full 17 days of competition, agencies from around the world were in attendance to report on the second largest sporting event next to the Summer Olympics.

More than 2,300 reporters, photographers, radio announcers, television commentators and technical support staff helped bring the Pan Am Games to an estimated audience of 400 million worldwide. And while the Pan Am Games

186

VOLUNTEERS

only include athletes from the Americas, there was still media presence from 25 "foreign" countries, including agencies from China, India, Spain and Germany.

The Canadian Broadcasting Corporation (CBC) served as the host broadcaster of the Games and provided the signal to Canadian television and radio rights holders such as the CBC network, NetStar Communications (TSN - The Sports Network/RDS) and WIC Radio. It also provided the signal to radio and television rights holders in Latin America and the Caribbean, as well as to Spanish language cable networks throughout North America.

The Panasonic International Broadcast Centre was located at the CBC Studios in Winnipeg. The CBC and TSN teamed up to broadcast 100 hours of Pan Am programming, approximately 35 hours of prime coverage by CBC which included Opening and Closing Ceremonies. During prime time hours the CBC drew audiences of up to 576,000, a viewer number that matches the average audience of a Toronto Blue Jays baseball game. The CBC however, managed to capture that audience for 17 consecutive nights. TSN provided afternoon coverage, drawing a solid audience of 100,000 as a consistent daytime rating, an impressive number for a cable company network. With a focus on Manitoba's own, additional Games coverage was seen locally every night on CBC Manitoba and its Northwest Ontario repeater stations.

Local Winnipeg cable companies produced programming as well, enabling Manitoba cable customers to tune in for the most up to date information on ticket availability, daily events and competitions, nightly entertainment line-ups at the Forks and transportation information which included free parking areas, ride locations and street closures.

The print side of the media played a tremendous role in the coverage and promotion of the Games as well. Compelling features, captivating images and noteworthy results appeared daily in the Winnipeg Free Press, the Globe and Mail, the National Post, the Edmonton Sun, the Toronto Sun and the Winnipeg Sun. The Winnipeg Free Press demonstrated its commitment to the Games and the Winnipeg community with a daily "Pan Am Section" that wrapped the outside of the daily's regular section. Many big name American newspapers also surfaced during the Games including The New York Times, the Los Angeles Times, The Miami Herald and the Washington Post. And a number of leading magazines had their names on the media roster as well, a list topped by Sports Illustrated, ESPN Magazine, Tennis Week, Newsweek, Maclean's and People Magazine.

Winnipeg was playing in the sports world's big leagues and it did not disappoint. Together with The Document Company - Xerox, Winnipeg's Pan Am Games Society assembled one of the finest big-event Press Centres, driven by knowledgeable, accommodating and amicable staff. "We knew we would have cream of the crop accredited journalists and photographers at the Games," stated George Einarson, Media Services Manager for the event. "We researched and

LASTING IMPRESSIONS

THE FOOD IS GOOD, PEOPLE ARE FRIENDLY, BUSES ARE RUNNING ON TIME AND PERHAPS MOST IMPORTANTLY, THE BEER IS CHEAP. FOR THE MOST PART, THIS WAS THE RESPONSE FROM FOREIGN JOURNALISTS WHEN ASKED WHAT THEY THOUGHT OF WINNIPEG AND THE JOB THE CITY DID IN HOSTING THE PAN AM GAMES. "THE FIRST THING YOU NOTICE IS THE HOSPITALITY OF THE PEOPLE," OBSERVED MIKE DODD, A USA TODAY REPORTER AND VETERAN OF FOUR OLYMPIC GAMES. "THAT'S WHAT MAKES AN EVENT LIKE THIS SPECIAL."

VOLUNTEERS

studied what type of equipment and services would be needed to accommodate the press."

The Xerox Main Press Centre occupied a significant section of the second floor of the Winnipeg Convention Centre. It was the 24-hour media headquarters where the accredited media had the means to cover, prepare and file stories for the worldwide audience. The press centre was equipped with 266 workstations complete with phones and modem adapters for instantaneous reporting. A medley of 23 televisions offered off-air feeds so reporters could accurately describe the action as it happened at the venues, even if the event wasn't being televised, and then forward immediate information back to their home base.

Together, the Xerox Main Press Centre, the venues and the athlete villages, provided work for 721 volunteers, responsible for the sometimes onerous task of dealing directly with the media. Each venue had a media sub-centre, a tent set up strictly for media, where members had access to similar researching, viewing and story filing services as those found in the main centre. A generally harmonious working relationship between media and volunteers, Einarson reported that, "Some volunteers even made sandwiches for the media." He wasn't surprised at such hospitality. "We gathered the best people our province had to offer to look after the media," Einarson pledged. "Manitoba's friendly spirit is what made the Games 32 years ago a success and that same spirit thrived once again during the 1999 Games."

SHARING THE DREAM

Long before the Opening Ceremony, before Pan A'mania had taken hold of the city, Sport Manitoba had been building the foundation for a Games legacy. By bringing local athletes to area school events, Sport Manitoba and the Pan Am organizing committee not only increased the profile of Manitoba's Pan Am-bound athletes and their achievements, but also gave some exposure and identity to lesser known sports. All the while they were creating an excitement about the Games within the province's youth.

Instrumental in this programming was Suzanne St. Jorge, Special Events Coordinator for Sport Manitoba. She launched Athletes in the Schools - Sharing the Dream. "We really wanted to get kids more involved in sport now, spurring them on to become involved in the future," explained St. Jorge. Not surprisingly, schools embraced the spirit behind the program.

Athletes spent about an hour at a school, often accompanied by Pato or Lorita, the official mascots of the Winnipeg Pan Am Games. Children received locker cards from the athletes to commemorate their visit. Some presentations saw athletes perform demonstrations of their events, complete with proper equipment and a show of medals won from previous competitions. The children relished the opportunity to interact with the athletes. "We

188

"I've always tended to call on people I know when I get involved in a volunteer program, but working with all these ne and wonderful people may be my most memorable experience of the Games." *Joan MacDonald, Spectator Servic*

tried to get athletes who were on the Pan Am Track," expressed St. Jorge in reference to competitors expected to qualify for the Games. "But we didn't limit it there; there are many other athletes out there who have done great things but are not necessarily Pan Am athletes."

Although the program was meant to spark interest in sport, unexpected educational aspects presented themselves. "We had local wrestler Mike Smith involved," St. Jorge smiled. "He was constantly inundated with questions about the WWF (World Wrestling Federation). He made a point of trying to explain the differences between wrestling as a sport and wrestling as entertainment, describing how the point structure works, the scoring, etceteras. Mike enforced the idea that this isn't something to fool around with in the schoolyard. He really helped to clear up a lot of the misconceptions about the sport."

The program was initially targeted at kids from grades four to six, but in the end kids from kindergarten up to grade nine had exposure to it. St. Jorge noted that a minimal starting budget was to allow for presentations at 30 schools. "We ended up doing 82 schools, 41 within the city and 41 outside," St. Jorge detailed. "We were able to get athletes out to remote regions, areas that might not get to see many athletes up close and in the flesh." The program adopted 15 athletes, reaching over 19,800 Manitoban students in a five month period. "Having the Games in the city will increase our youth's involvement in organized sport, if not as an athlete, maybe as an official or a coach," St. Jorge surmised confidently.

DOCUMENTING CANADA'S LARGEST SPORTING EVENT

The athletes competing at the Winnipeg '99 Pan American Games earned our respect and admiration because of their ability to do two things at once: reach for individual excellence, while working with a team, coaches, trainers and fellow athletes. The Document Company - Xerox is much like those athletes. Xerox is the world leader in digital document management services and solutions - forever striving to be at the forefront of technology and customer solutions. But Xerox has achieved its leadership position through a long history of co-operation with its business partners, clients and the communities it serves.

More than 100 Xerox employees across Canada were directly involved with the Games, from designing the document management strategy to supporting the 1,100 pieces of Xerox equipment installed to meet the Games' document requirements. Many more Xerox employees volunteered their personal time to ensure the Games were a success.

That included 1,000 hours of overtime on evenings and weekends during which every piece of equipment was individually tested to verify it was in full working order. The service dedication paid off - the equipment worked virtually trouble-free and gave the Games the quality service required to be a success. For any problems that did arise, 50 Xerox service representatives were on-hand at the Operations Centre from six a.m. until two a.m. every day. "If any technical problems occurred, we could have someone on a site in as little as two minutes," recalled Bob Perreault,

VOLUNTEERS

Customer Service Operations Manager for Xerox.

Documenting the Pan Am Games was a difficult task and we needed to overcome a number of hurdles, said Marlene Smart, Pan Am Games Project Manager for Xerox. Smart was responsible for accommodating the information needs of the 125,000 tourists, 18,000 volunteers and 2,000 journalists that attended the 17-day event. "Just like the athletes competing here, the process to produce each document had to possess several attributes: speed, accuracy, and excellence."

The backdrop to these challenges was the continual need to minimize costs, uphold strict environmental practices and serve the special needs of the Games. Xerox met each challenge with the determination of a gold medallist. Due to the magnitude and scope of the Pan Am Games, The Document Company assigned Smart as Project Manager in 1997 - two years before the first pop of a starter's pistol. Xerox trained hard for over two years to ensure all materials, including rule books, training guides and event results were printed and ready for spectators and the international press corps at the Xerox Main Press Centre. Virtually every document printed was available in all three official languages of the Games - English, French and Spanish.

There was a lot at stake. An estimated 35 million documents were published and distributed by the time the last athlete in the last competition crossed the finish line. But the volume of documents produced was merely one challenge. Greater still was the need to publish many of these documents in less time than it takes a gold medallist to sprint 100 metres.

"Xerox provided us with more than print technologies," said Jerry Maslowsky, Vice President of Communications, Promotions and Media Services for the Games. "They delivered the know-how and expertise to manage our documents. In essence they were there at every event."

As important as it is for elite athletes to have the physical strength to succeed in competition, equally significant is a keen sense of strategy. This was no less true for those supplying information technology solutions to the Games. It was with strategy and service in mind that Smart enlisted Xerox Global Document Services (XGDS), The Document Company's consulting and outsourcing arm, to lend their expertise to the Games. Terry Watling, Customer Operations Manager for XGDS, and his team brought their knowledge gained from working on complex and demanding engagements across Canada and around the world to play a vital role on the Xerox team.

Xerox also coordinated its efforts with organizers and other suppliers to develop a remarkably efficient and cost-effective way to create and distribute documents. The results are a testament to global teamwork. Kevin Francis, President, Chairman and CEO of Xerox Canada Ltd. likened Xerox' experience to a relay race. "We were on the same team, working together in a fast-paced environment. Xerox' job was to pass on its expertise and solutions to the organizers and let them run with it."

VOLUNTEERS

It was wonderful meeting the families of some of the players. I befriended one couple who were at every beach volleyball game. I saw them after the gold medal game. The lady had bouquet of flowers. Her daughter won a medal. She said thank you to the volunteers for 'being so kind and helpful.' Our motto was to never say 'it's not my job.' *Culver A. Warr*

Keith Levit

TECHNOLOGY BEHIND THE GAMES

Cutting-edge technology from Panasonic helped set the stage and capture the drama of one of the world's great sports spectacles, the 1999 Pan American Games. While the players and heroes of this 17-day epic - an elite cast of 5,000 athletes representing 42 countries - wrote the script for the final Pan American Games of this millennium, Panasonic as Official Partner of the Games, played the lead role in bringing to the world some of the most incredible scenes in sports. The multimillion-dollar Panasonic International Broadcast Centre served as the electronic crossroads of the XIII Pan Am Games in Winnipeg, with a top team of technicians recording and broadcasting all of the action during 41 sports competitions. The Broadcast Centre's sophisticated audio and video equipment supplied direct feeds to 23 international broadcast companies, including the CBC and TSN in Canada. An estimated 150 million viewers tuned into the games in North and South America alone.

VOLUNTEERS

The Broadcast Centre - a tiny city in itself, encompassing several buildings, 27 trailers and 81,000 square feet of space - showcased some of the most exciting new technology on the planet. The lineup of equipment included more than 36 DVCPRO digital videotape machines, nine ENG camcorder units and more than 40 colour monitors.

Beyond the Broadcast Centre, Panasonic equipped some 50 sites in and around the Games - from the Athletes' Village to VIP hotels and the Winnipeg Convention Centre - with 1,000 pieces of consumer electronic equipment, including TVs, VCRs, camcorders, CD players and tape decks. In the Athletes' Village, the stars of these 1999 Games, the athletes who spent years preparing and training for their moment on the world stage, watched Panasonic TV monitors to keep up with all of the televised coverage.

Keith Levit

VOLUNTEERS

Panasonic also provided the closed-circuit TV surveillance security system used in the Village and throughout the Games venues to ensure safety and assist police and security teams. And of course, Panasonic's two giant Astrovision television displays made sure that everyone at the Games caught a breathtaking view of each competition.

Keith Levit

The Astrovision screens, already used to wide acclaim during major sporting events like the Atlanta and Nagano Olympics and the U.S. college football classic the Rose Bowl, made their Canadian debut at the 1999 Games. Two Astrovision screens, each measuring 20-by-25 feet, were situated at key locations during the Games, giving spectators a faultless sight line on all the action. One Astrovision screen was used at the Royal Bank Stage situated at the Forks, the focal point of the Games' colourful lineup of cultural events and entertainment. The second screen, a mobile unit, was placed in Winnipeg Stadium for the thrilling opening ceremony, then moved to the University of Manitoba's Athletic Stadium during the Games before landing back in Winnipeg Stadium for the unforgettable closing ceremonies.

For Panasonic, the Official Partner of these Games, more than a year of planning and strategy sessions were held prior to the first equipment arriving in Winnipeg for installing and testing in March - five months before the Games. Just the cables alone used to link up the impressive electronic setup for the Games spanned 24 miles in all! To wring maximum performance from all the high-tech broadcast and monitoring equipment, Panasonic assembled a top-flight team of all star technicians from Canada, the United States and Japan. In all, Panasonic's technical, marketing and sales staff numbered about 50. Of course, the XIII Pan Am Games proved to be just the latest challenge for Panasonic, a company with a growing tradition of participating in the world's biggest sports competitions.

Panasonic has been an official worldwide Olympic Games sponsor since 1988, as well as Security supplier to the 1994 Commonwealth Games in Victoria, B.C. In 1995 and 1996, the company was Official Partner to Canada's National Rowing Teams, and for two years leading up to the 1998 Winter Olympics, sponsored the Canadian National Snowboard Team.

The exciting link to sports continues: Panasonic's parent company, Matsushita Electrical Industrial Co. Ltd., has already signed a contract with the Sydney Olympic Broadcasting Organization to become official host broadcast equipment supplier for the 2000 Summer Olympic Games in Sydney. Panasonic is thrilled by the prospect of setting the stage once more for an unforgettable sports epic, and bringing it to the world as a new millennium begins.

| 193

Keith Levit

VOLUNTEERS

PAN AM MEMORY Kim Ferguson, Winnipeg

My husband and I could not let our encounter with a Jamaican athlete go unnoticed - it was our Pan Am highlight by far. Our three-year-old son jumped on the pin-collecting craze and we wanted to get him a Cayman Island pin (turtle) and we weren't having much luck. So we decided to go to the CFB athlete village and stand outside hoping to meet a Cayman athlete. While we were standing there, a Jamaican athlete was entering the village and saw our son's T-shirt filled with pins and immediately felt his pocket for a pin. He did not have one on him. He apologized, then he said that he would go to his room and get one for him and that we should wait. Now it wasn't just a short jaunt, it was a long walk.

About 15 minutes later, as he said, he came back with a Jamaican pin for our son! He went way out of his way just so that our son could have another pin for his collection. Everyone at that gate was amazed and very impressed by his actions. It made us all feel great to have this encounter. I did not get his name, but were so impressed by his ambassadorship for his country. Not to be outdone, a dignitary from Barbados also didn't have a pin and went and borrowed one from one of his countrymen to give to our son. The Games were not only about who won gold, silver or bronze medals. Thet were happenings behind the scenes that made this an experience that we will never forget. I thank them both deeply.

HOT STUFF

When the dust of Winnipeg's Pan Am Games settled, slightly more than $800,000 worth of official merchandise had flown off the shelves during the two-week Games period. Coupled with the incredible sales run of Pan Am products in the years leading up to the event, retail merchandise sales totalled more than $10 million. That translates to more than $600,000 in royalties to the Pan Am Games Society.

From giant pencils and magic cubes to T-shirts and plush toys, Pan Am stuff was hot. Winnipeg retailer Boes Ltd. was the official merchandise concessionnaire at the Games but exceptional retail support from major outlets like the Bay, as well as a host of committed independent specialty store, pushed merchandise sales passed the organizing committee's original expectations by $4 million.

While the revenue was tremendous, Dwight Embleton, Pan Am Games Merchandise Licensing Manager, noted that the strength of the licensing program went beyond the revenue for the organizing committee. "It was also about the exposure for the Games and the enthusiasm that it created," he remarked. "When I started seeing

Ken Gigliott

people in different parts of the country wearing Winnipeg '99 T-shirts, I knew Pan Am products were a hit."

The success of the merchandise was also related to its positioning in the marketplace. A range in pricing - you could buy an item for as little as $5.00 or as much as $360 with melton-leather jackets at the high end - provided something for everyone. The quality of the products, and the popularity of the Games logo and mascot, contributed to the fashionableness of the merchandise.

An assortment of 12 licensees, the majority Winnipeg-based, produced the array of souvenirs. Among the keychains, glassware, calendars, caps, sweatshirts and other apparel, the best seller was the smallest item available. Laurie Artiss, the Regina-based pin licensee, churned out more than 500,000 lapel pins. One of the more interesting licensees came to Embleton as a community project presented by two Red River College Business Administration students. The company, Emanate Marketing, developed and marketed juggling sticks called Mystiks that were sold at venue concessions. What was Embleton's greatest challenge as merchandise manager? "Keeping product in stock," he smiled. He credited an outstanding team of licensees for ensuring the success of the merchandise program. "Some of these companies worked day and night to meet the demand for Pan Am products during the Games," he commended.

SIMPLE ECONOMICS FROM AN ECONOMIC PERSPECTIVE, HOSTING THE PAN AM GAMES SHOULD PROVE TO BE VERY BENEFICIAL FOR WINNIPEG AND THE WHOLE OF CANADA. WINNIPEG AND THE REST OF THE COUNTRY HAD THE ATTENTION OF VISITORS FROM ALL CORNERS OF THE WESTERN HEMISPHERE. THE IMMEDIATE ECONOMIC BENEFITS INCLUDED AN EXPECTED $28.5 MILLION IN EXPENDITURES IN MANITOBA OVER THE COURSE OF THE GAMES. MEASURABLY, THE GAMES INCREASED TOURISM, PROVIDED JOBS, AND CONTRIBUTED TO THE CANADIAN ECONOMY. BUT LOOKING BEYOND THE GAMES, THIS TYPE OF INTERNATIONAL EXPOSURE WILL ALMOST CERTAINLY FACILITATE THE PROMOTION OF INCREASED TRADE AND INVESTMENT WELL INTO THE NEW MILLENNIUM.

PREVENTATIVE MEDICINE

The heat kept them busy. There were incidents of scrapes and abrasions too. But predominantly, there was a whole lot of preventative medicine administered. Next to the army of Games volunteers, they were likely the most diverse team at the Pan Ams. They were St. John Ambulance's brigade of volunteers, a collection of seasoned and newly-trained personnel on hand to attend to, and divert, medical emergencies at the venues.

Led by Jane Hook, St. John Ambulance Pan Am Games Coordinator, the team of 460 had representation from every Canadian province, from England and as far away as Australia. In fact, responsible for their own expenses to and from Winnipeg, the contingent from England competed for the chance to win the St. John spots at the Games. Hook said that St. John's existing volunteer base was complemented by an assembly of individuals who responded to a public appeal from the organization. Respondees received a two-day training course at no cost and Standard First Level certification from St. John Ambulance. Over 350 new certificates were issued. Hook noted that the complimentary certification was not completely altruistic. "We hope they'll continue with us as volunteers," she opined. "If nothing else, we've provided a legacy to the community, with 350 more people with CPR skills for their daily lives and those around them."

TRAINING THE TRAINER

Ten of Manitoba's up-and-coming coaches had an opportunity for advanced training and major games coaching experience through the 1999 Pan American Games Coaching Apprenticeship Program. A joint initiative of the Pan American Games Society, Sport Manitoba, the National Coaching Institute - Manitoba, the Coaching Association of Canada, Canadian Olympic Association and Canadian Heritage (Sport Canada), the Apprenticeship Program gave Manitoba coaches the chance to work with Canadian teams participating in the 1999 Pan American Games. The Pan Am Games Society provided $25,000 in funding for the program; Sport Manitoba contributed $15,000. The Coaching Association of Canada granted $40,000 specifically for female coaches as part of their Women in Coaching initiatives.

Up to $5,000 in financial assistance was made available to each Manitoba coach in the program. Apprenticeship coaches served as regular members of their respective team staff, involved in pre-competitive training, team selection activities, and competition and training camp schedules leading up to the Games. The program's objective was to help prepare them for future coaching opportunities with national teams and international competitive events.

IN THE SPIRIT OF ABORIGINAL TRADITION

Under the direction of Jeff Ross, Aboriginal Liaison Officer with the Pan Am Games Society, strategies, concepts and programs were developed to maximize the participation of Manitoba's Aboriginal community during the Games. One of the first initiatives was the creation of an Aboriginal Advisory Committee to assist Ross with the involvement of the Metis and First Nation Community. "We involved community members from all walks of life to maximize opportunities for Aboriginals in all areas of the Games," said Ross. "We wanted Aboriginals to participate right across the board," he said.

The Aboriginal Mentorship Program hired 11 Aboriginals, one for each division within the Games Society, to assist with projects and gain valuable experience in career development, networking and self-discipline. "When Winnipeg hosts the North American Indigenous Games in 2002, these candidates could become the core people on the organizing committee," Ross explained.

Ross revealed that when he reviewed the history of the Games, particularly the 1967 Games in Winnipeg, he found very little Aboriginal participation in the Opening and Closing Ceremonies. Ross worked closely with the vice-president of Festivals to ensure a strong Aboriginal presence for the ceremonies and the festivals associated with the Games. This presence involved the Tribal Journey, gift ceremonies, volunteers, an internship program with CBC, the host broadcaster, and a cultural village which was erected on a site at The Forks, with people recreating the activities of the original Red River settlement.

AN ANISHINAABE HONOUR FOR PRINCESS ANNE PAN AM GAMES ROYAL GUEST PRINCESS ANNE RECEIVED THE ABORIGINAL NAME OGIMAAKWENS FROM MEMBERS OF THE ANISHINAABE NATION DURING A TRADITIONAL NATIVE CEREMONY AT THE ABORIGINAL CENTRE IN WINNIPEG DURING THE GAMES. LOOSELY TRANSLATED AS CHIEF PRINCESS, THE NEWLY NAMED OGIMAAKWENS SAT AMONGST A GROUP OF ABOUT 150 PEOPLE WITH A HANDFUL OF ABORIGINAL ELDERS. QUEEN VICTORIA WAS THE FIRST TO BE HONOURED WITH AN ANISHINAABE NAME, AFTER TREATIES WERE SIGNED DURING HER REIGN. SHE WAS GIVEN THE NAME GICHI OGIMAA KWE, MEANING SUPREME LEADER OF THE CROWN.

VOLUNTEERS

"I was asked to head up the whole media accreditation area, putting the whole thing together, planning the layout, training the volunteers. I'm sort of a compulsive volunteer to begin with. I thought, if something this exciti was going on in the city, I wanted to be a part of it. My favourite part of the job was meeting the people from different countries, and learning a little bit of Spanish." *Marnie Strath, Coordinator of Media Accreditation Cen*

A LASTING IMPRESSION

The Pan American Games Society knew how to make an impression. And the judges for the annual Signature Advertising Awards are not impressed easily. Winnipeg's Pan Am organizing committee captured seven out of 11 Signature Awards before the Games for its public awareness campaign. The Signature Awards recognize excellence in advertising in Manitoba.

The panel of judges consists of individuals from the advertising industry throughout Canada. The committee's trophy haul included Best Single Television Commercial Award, Best Direct Mail Award, Best Television Series Award, Best Multimedia Campaign Award, Best Television Award, Best of Show Award and the Best of the Rest Award.

Awards aside, the advertising campaign achieved its objective, voiced Richard Muller, vice-president of Image and Creative Services for the Pan Am Games. "Ongoing tracking research indicated that 98 per cent of people in Winnipeg and 87 per cent of the people in urban areas were aware of the Games long before the athletes arrived." With television, billboards, radio and bus boards in their media fold, the world-class awareness campaign featured larger than life athletes performing their sport in and upon famous Winnipeg and Manitoba landmarks. "It gave the XIIIth Pan Am Games a sense of place - of where they would be held," Muller specificated.

VOLUNTEERS

PAN AM MEAL TIME

Games Food Services worked hard to feed 7,000 hungry athletes, coaches, trainers and mission staff. Here's a slice of what they served up.

- 400,000 meals
- 28,500 kilograms of chicken
- 13,600 kilograms of ribs
- 114,000 kilograms of apples
- 2.7 metric tonnes of pasta
- 1 million cookies
- 320,000 wieners (48 kilometres of hot dogs!)

- 9,500 litres of ketchup portions
- 18,000 kilograms of french fries
- 135,000 kilograms of ice per day
- 16,000 loaves of bread
- 1/2 million eggs
- 61,200 kilograms of vegetables
- 1.2 million bottled waters distributed to athletes, volunteers and staff

IN THE WAKE OF THE GAMES

In addition to the experience that the 1999 Pan American Games provided to the competing athletes, the event will also provide the Winnipeg region with an important sport legacy of world-class facilities to be used in the development of the next generation of athletes. Wherever possible the new facilities will be available for multiple uses after the Games. This will benefit the National Sport Centre located in Winnipeg making the region an attractive training and competition centre for Canadian athletes.

Keith Levit

Perhaps the most impressive physical legacy left to the community following the Games is the Investors Group Athletic Centre. The creation of the $8.6 million building was a team effort. Three levels of government, the University of Manitoba and Investors Group worked together to establish this world-class facility. The naming of the building as the Investors Group Athletic Centre was in recognition of the contributions Investors

VOLUNTEERS

Group had made to the University over the years.

The 70,000 square-foot gymnasium features three courts for basketball and volleyball, dressing rooms, an athletic therapy centre and over 3,500 spectator seats. The multi-purpose complex played host to basketball, volleyball and rhythmic gymnastics during the Games. "The Investors Group Athletic Centre will be a legacy for generations to come," said Don MacKenzie, President and CEO of the Pan Am Games Society.

Like the Pan Am Pool, the most significant legacy of the 1967 Games, a top-notch baseball stadium and artificial-turf field hockey venue fill out the list of facilities that will remain as a legacy in the community long after the 1999 Pan American Games. CanWest Global Park, a 5,700-seat baseball stadium situated just north of The Forks in the heart of downtown Winnipeg, is the new home of the Winnipeg Goldeyes Baseball Club of the Northern League. It was utilized for the Pan Am baseball tournament. Goldeyes' owner Sam Katz ensured that the ballpark will be "an important athletic, entertainment and gathering place for the community for a long time to come." The Pan Am field hockey venue, a first-rate artificial turf facility at the East Side Eagles Field, will remain as a multi-use recreational area for local amateur sport teams, particularly football, field hockey, baseball, soccer and lacross.

With a balanced Games budget, the sporting community in the province will be left with a legacy of sports equipment as well. Top-of-the-line balls and nets and timing systems will nurture the next generation of athletes. A Games-end budget in the black will secure a financial contribution from the Host Society to Manitoba's National Sport Centre located in Winnipeg. Strong ticket and merchandising sales, healthy sponsorship and careful expense management all but guaranteed a legacy for the National Sport Centre at Games end.

The National Sport Centre - Manitoba is dedicated to the support of athletic excellence by providing programs and services for Manitoba's high performance athletes. The Pan Am legacy would assist the Centre in providing greater access to services for "athletes on the bubble," in reference to those athletes striving for national or international positions. Alex Gardiner, the Centre's General Manager, hopes to utilize the excess funds from the Games to institute new programs to assist athletes and coaches in their athletic development as they "reach for new heights." The legacy fund would also allow for more coaching scholarships. "Ultimately," explained Gardiner, "we'd like to attract more national teams to Winnipeg for full-time residency, training camps and tournaments, all of which will expose more Manitoba athletes to elite-level competition."

Bricks and mortar, balls and bats aside, the Games left some priceless intangibles in its wake as well. The Pan Ams provided valuable experience to some 20,000 volunteers and Games staff. This infusion of opportunity will likely improve the skills, talents, expertise and confidence within Winnipeg's professional and volunteer sectors that will serve the community long into the future.

VOLUNTEERS

PAN AM STAMPS

It's a world of high standards: first issues, special cancellations and limited runs. They're considered miniature masterpieces by philatelists and it is the most popular hobby in the world; stamp collecting is serious business for aficionados. On July 12, 1999 Canada Post introduced a set of four stamps in association with the XIIIth Pan American Games.

Designed by a collaborative team at Circle Design Incorporated of Winnipeg, the creators faced a conundrum from the very start. How do you represent 41 sports on four stamps that measure a mere 36 by 36 millimetres in size? "We categorized them into water-based sports, track and field, team sports and endurance and strength related sports," explained Jeff Peterson of Circle Design. "Our goal was to be as broadly representative as possible." Each of the stamps has three scenarios with a dominant scene in the middle and two smaller background images, which are muted. "The idea of personal endeavour, strength, tenacity and spirit were the drivers that we looked at when we began to draw the stamps," he said.

"The process of designing a stamp is really quite interesting," remarked Carissa Romans of Circle Design. "It comes down to portraying ideas accurately on only a tiny canvas." The firm was selected by Canada Post through a concept contest open to design firms. A selection panel at Canada Post chose from a variety of renderings. Once settled on the images, Winnipeg artist Andrew Valko was commissioned to bring the concepts to life.

"Canada's stamps have the highest reproduction standards in the world," expressed Peterson. "It's an interesting process because it invloves security printing so that every sheet of paper is numbered and accounted for. The press itself is inside a large cage that is fully monitored. There are only two printers in Canada licensed to print stamps and money." Besides the stamps them-

selves, the designers also worked on the special cancellations and the first-day covers, both of which are standard for Canada Post stamps. Since the stamps were so successful, Canada Post also commissioned a poster, postcards and a set of four pins for the Games. The poster had two purposes, said Rosanne Spence of Canada Post. "One is as an autograph collector so that the athletes could keep it as a souvenir of the Games. The other is as a purely philatelic product."

Of the three special cancellations that were developed for the Games, one was available only at the athlete villages, setting up an exclusivity which is highly sought after by collectors. "There are a lot of folks who are very fanatical about getting the special cancellations on things," Peterson said.

Peterson spoke of an implicit satisfaction in designing something that is so exacting but also treasured by its community. "Stamps are interesting because they have very dedicated and expert communities that attach themselves to them," he described. "Stamps can be viewed as ambassadors. They act as little messengers about Canada, about the values and lifestyle and the things we enjoy here because they're sent all over the world." Peterson went on to say: "In an age of virtual presence and communications that is often not very tactile, not very substantive, there's something about a stamp that has this precious little artifact aspect to it. It is fun creating things like that and knowing that they are appreciated is gratifying."

VOLUNTEERS

"Sports and culture bring people together in a special and personal way.

Watching athletes and artists perform together on the Pan American

stage in Winnipeg reached beyond language and cultural differences, cre-

ating a sense of community and shared values."

MINISTER OF FOREIGN AFFAIRS LLOYD AXWORTHY

CULTURAL FESTIVAL

WINNIPEG WITH THE LIGHTS ON

Long ago, before the Games began, the chairman of the board of director's for the 1999 Pan Am Games remarked that he wanted his kids to see Winnipeg "with the lights on," like it had in 1967 when he was a boy. Sandy Riley's wish came true. The Forks, dubbed MTS Canada Place for the Games, was a flurry of activity day and night. Located at the geographic centre of the Games, the historic landing was the cultural heart and soul of the Games. Free performances on any one of four stages during the day, street performers, and a wide range of cultural and historic exhibits provided plenty to choose from. The night time festivities began with the Centra Gas Game Day Highlights on the

203

Panasonic Astrovision screen, followed by free nightly concerts on the Royal Bank Stage. Nearly every evening, the celebrations ended with the "Flying Colours" fireworks displays presented by Ford.

THE HEART OF A CONTINENT

For about six thousand years, the site that is now Winnipeg was an important aboriginal trading centre in the heart of the continent. At the fork of two major rivers - the Assiniboine running east-west and the Red running north-south - aboriginal people from all over North America met to do business. Wyoming obsidian was traded for Lake Superior copper; Dakota flint was exchanged for Hudson Bay spear point.

In 1738, French explorer and fur trader La Verendrye built Fort Rouge at the rivers' confluence. For the next 75 years, the site was a busy fur trading centre. In 1812, the Red River colony under Lord Selkirk settled at the site.

As the Canadian Pacific Railway pushed across Canada in the late 1800s, the strategic bifurcation of the Red and Assiniboine Rivers was once again a natural focus for development. Winnipeg was founded in 1873, and for a few

VOLUNTEERS

decades was the fastest-growing city in North America. As the west was opened, Winnipeg was the central depot for people and cargo moving east and west, north and south. Winnipeg's Exchange District, a 30-block area, presents a living snapshot of the boom period from 1881 to 1918.

Winnipeg is poised to play an important role in the new millennium as a gateway along the Mid-Continent International Trade Corridor. The corridor is an evolving new trade pattern - a band of interconnecting highways, railways, air and information routes stretching through the centre of the continent, from Mexico to Hudson Bay. At its heart stands Winnipeg, once again a trading hub as it has been for millennia.

WHERE THE AMERICAS CAME TO PERFORM

Set into the background of the bustling Forks, the Royal Bank Stage hosted a melange of performances during the Games. For 15 nights, performers from all artistic disciplines and every imaginable musical genre delighted capacity audiences. From the grassroots sounds of Great Big Sea to the internationally acclaimed Neville Brothers, the nightly

free concerts were a welcome distraction from the suspense of the day's competitions. Embraced by Minister of Foreign Affairs Lloyd Axworthy, the stage welcomed crowds of over 30,000 each night, with several nights spilling over 60,000 to go down as the largest concert audiences in Winnipeg's history.

Conspicuous from a distance with its bright blue frame and pink perimeter, the music resonated out from the stage and over the entire Forks area urging the festivities to continue late into the night. The venue showcased different themes each evening, accentuating the diverse cultures and traditions of the Pan American countries.

Running the stage required a substantial backbone of volunteers, anywhere between 45 to 55 each evening, to ensure the staged events ran smoothly. Coordinated by Gwenda Coombs, Royal Bank's volunteer team consisted of company employees, family members and pensioners, totalling just over 400.

Each night's performances were enhanced through the Panasonic Astrovision Screen, measuring over seven metres in height. A fireworks display set to music, compliments of Ford Motor Company, capped off most evenings. The eclectic line-up of entertainers provided something for everyone, if not within the course of an evening, certainly over the course of the Games. Each night was devoted to a specific theme, with a diversity of acts, including dance, classical music, pop, jazz, country and western, rock, folk and multi-cultural performances.

Bruce Rapinchuk

VOLUNTEERS

GREATEST HITS

Each night of the Pan Am cultural festival had a theme, more or less. The main stage line-up brought together the best of the Americas across a broad spectrum of musical styles and formats.

OPENING NIGHT: Fubuki Daiko, Chai Folk Ensemple, Danzamerica, Blue Rodeo

CLASSICAL NIGHT: Saxology, Silvio Solis, Winnipeg Symphony Orchestra, Finjan

FRANCOPHONE NIGHT: L'ensemble Folklorique de la Riviere Rouge, Annie Berthiaume, Dubmatique

SOUTH AMERICAN NIGHT: Licanantay, Norteno, Tangomaria, Diego Marulanda and Pacande

CELTIC NIGHT: Scruj Macduhk, Cascabulho, Great Big Sea

ABORIGINAL NIGHT: Los Imbayakunas, Xipe Tote, Red Bone

COUNTRY NIGHT: Country Hearts, Paul Brandt

JAZZ NIGHT: Walle Larsson, Javier Enrique, Johnny Favourite Swing Orchestra

CARIBBEAN-CANADIAN NIGHT: Caraballo, Spank Band & Nita, Frankie Wilmot

DANCE NIGHT: Rusalka, Winnipeg Contemporary Dancers, Neo Labos, Delphos, The Stars of Canadian Ballet

CENTRAL AMERICAN NIGHT: Grupo Sabor, Osvaldo Ayala, B.C. Salsa

CARIBBEAN NIGHT: Grenada National Folk Group, Tobago Heritage Folk Performers, Square One

INTERNATIONAL NIGHT: Jane Bunnett, Jimmy Cliff, First Nations Hoop Dancers, Neville Brothers

ROCK NIGHT: Spur of The Moment, Wilfrido Vargas, Philosopher Kings

MANITOBA NIGHT: Chantal Kreviazuk, Danny Kramer, Royal Winnipeg Ballet, McMaster & James, Larry Roy

A COMMITMENT TO DIVERSITY

Foreign Affairs Minister Lloyd Axworthy and Manitoba Minister of Northern and Native Affairs, David Newman, gave $650,000 in federal/provincial support for an ambitious Tribal Canoe Journey from York Factory to Winnipeg and the establishment of an Aboriginal Cultural Village at the Forks National Historic Site during the Pan Am Games. The projects assisted Manitoba's First Nation and Metis community in the promotion of their heritage, culture and spirit during the Games. "As Canada prepared to open its arms to representatives of 42 countries we also ensured the Aboriginal community had a prominent role in the extraordinary cultural celebrations that characterized these Games," said Minister Axworthy. "Not only did the Tribal Journey and Cultural Village further enrich the Pan Am experience for the Aboriginal community and visitors to Winnipeg, these projects also gave us an opportunity to promote Manitoba's role as host of the 2002 North American Indigenous Games."

The Aboriginal Cultural Village highlighted traditional forms of dress, crafts, foods and games. A range of

VOLUNTEERS

Aboriginal talent hailed from throughout the Americas performed on the Village's main and side stages. The Cultural Village featured a 12.5-metre high teepee complete with historical artifacts, photographs of Aboriginal history, and artisans demonstrating traditional crafts such as quill working and beading.

An Elder from each of Manitoba's Aboriginal groups was regularly on hand to share experiences and knowledge. The village consisted of nine teepees in all: one representing the history of Manitoba's Metis people, one for the eight independent First Nations of Manitoba, and seven were designated for the seven tribal councils in the province. Visitors could try traditional food at the cafe and enjoy aboriginal entertainers from Canada, the USA, Mexico, and South America.

NEW CREATION PROJECT

In the true spirit of the Games, Winnipeg's Contemporary Dancers (WCD) brought the world to its feet with their collaborative production: The Pan American New Creation Project. WCD had been exploring international initiatives for

more than three years but The New Creation Project was the first significant international co-production of its nature. It was a celebration of the cultural and artistic diversity of the Pan American region and its artists.

Initiated by Tom Stroud, WCD's Artistic Director, the project's vision entailed integrating the various cultures involved in the Games without imposing on the project's development. Involved in the collaboration were Delfos Danza Contemporanea (Mexico) with choreographers Claudia Lavista and Victor Ruiz, Neo Labos Dancetheatre (United States) with choreographer Michele Elliman, and thirdly, WCD's choreographer Julia Sasso.

"It was a long standing vision that we had," expressed Stroud, "to use dance as a way to promote cultural exchange. We've been doing it with projects throughout Canada and the Pan Am Games provided us with a wonderful opportunity to explore the international arena."

The production was comprised of three pieces.

THE CANADA TREE
CREATED BY CANADIAN ARTIST
TYLER ASPIN, THE CANADA TREE
IS A MAGNIFICENT SCULPTURE
COMPOSED OF WOODS FROM
EACH CANADIAN PROVINCE AND
TERRITORY. SET WITHIN THIS
MOSAIC ARE ARTIFACTS THAT
TELL THE STORIES OF ORDINARY
AND EXTRAORDINARY
CANADIANS.

"Codex", by Neo Labos Dance Theatre, was based on the figurative movement sketches of Leonardo da Vinci and Calo Urbino and conceptualized in the spirit of the Pan American adventure. "Maa" by WCD, encompassed the writings of Octavio Paz: "divide: one man from another, one man from himself, they crumble ... we glimpse the unity that we lost ... the forgotten astonishment of being alive." The final piece, "No Existens Flores", by Delfos Danza Contemporanea, was inspired by the Mexican author Jaime Sabino. It delivered an intimate voyage through the emotions of love, eroticism and loneliness.

"The concept was to take dancers from the United States, Mexico and Canada to form one company," Stroud said. "We then took a choreographer from each country to create a new work in this newly formed group. We worked on trying to make sure the maximum amount of exchange and integration happened, so that in each of the new creations there was a mixture of dancers from each original company." A two-year endeavour, the structure included a three-week residency in Mexico, a four-week workshop staged in Winnipeg, followed by the final production performed at the Royal Bank Stage at The Forks during the first week of the Games. "Through the residencies, the teaching exchanges, the dialogue between the creators and the opportunity for our dancers to work with artists from other countries, the Pan American New Creation Project confirmed our belief that projects of this nature truly have the potential to reach beyond cultural differences," explained Stroud.

CELEBRATING A LEGACY OF ACHIEVEMENTS

Located in the heart of the bustling activity of The Forks was the Canada Place Pavilion, the feature Government of Canada display and information centre at the XIIIth Pan American Games. This dynamic interactive expo-style facility officially opened at the site of the future home of the Manitoba Theatre for Young People. Occupying over 900 square metres, the Pavilion offered Canadians and foreign visitors attending the Games a unique opportunity to experience the story of Canadian achievements both on and off the track. Billed as a celebration of Canadian identity, the interactive displays were meant to give the public a taste of what Canadians are accomplishing around the world while reminding us of our innovations at home. The Pavilion highlighted Canadian achievements in arts and culture, industry, heritage, diversity and international relations.

RCMP HISTORICAL VILLAGE

Visitors celebrated the heritage of the Royal Canadian Mounted Police, and had their photo taken with a Mountie on horseback of course, at the historical village. Visitors stepped back in time to 1874 with RCMP in period uniform and the Red Coats of the Northwest Mounted Police reenactment group. Displays of early firearms, included muskets, rifles, and a large cannon, were on site.

VOLUNTEERS

AN ADVENTURE IN DISCOVERY

Multi-dimensional. Multi-charactered. Multi-cultural. Winnipeg has all of the features that make an ideal urban centre. Winnipeg is a multi-ethnic city, and proud of it. Its ethnic fabric consists of Slavic, French, German, Native, Oriental, East Indian and Mediterranean traditions. And nowhere is this more evident than in the food the city offers.

From a perogy dinner in the North End to an asparagus and artichoke pizza on the Corydon Avenue strip, Winnipeg is chock full of unique dining experiences. Visitors can choose from a low-priced Ethiopian restaurant to an up-scale continental dining spot - and everything in between.

Winnipeg's diverse background is also reflected in its museums. The Manitoba Museum of Man and Nature can provide a whole day's entertainment, with its seven superbly-done galleries, as well as a full-size walk-on replica of the Nonsuch - a 17th century sailing ship that signaled the beginning of the fur-trade era. There's a children's museum, a prairie museum, a French Canadian museum, a Ukrainian museum and an aviation museum. Visitors can tour Ross House, the first post office west of the Great Lakes, or Dalnavert, the home of Hugh John Macdonald - former premier of Manitoba and son of Sir John A. Macdonald, the first prime minister of Canada.

Just as varied as its museums and its restaurants is Winnipeg's mix of the performing arts. There are no less than four main theatre companies, offering a variety of productions from Shakespeare to world premieres. In addition, there are several smaller groups specializing in children's and ethnic productions. Winnipeg is home to the Royal Winnipeg Ballet, Canada's oldest ballet company, and to the Winnipeg Symphony Orchestra. There's also the Manitoba Opera as well as the Contemporary Dancers and the Manitoba Chamber Orchestra. No less impressive than the performing arts scene is Winnipeg's wide choice of visual arts venues. The Winnipeg Art Gallery houses the largest collection of contemporary Inuit art in the world.

Green space is a part of Winnipeg's character and the city offers a variety of parks. The largest, Assiniboine Park, is also home to the Assiniboine Park Zoo. The Zoo features 1,200 live animals - and the statue of a very famous bear named after Winnipeg. Winnie-the Bear was a real bear, and is the basis of the children's storybook character, Winnie-the Pooh. Assiniboine Park is home to a one-of-a-kind garden as well. The Leo Mol Sculpture Garden features a number of bronze sculptures by world-renowned Winnipeg artist Leo Mol.

VOLUNTEERS

RESULTS

Produced for 330 medal ceremonies, there were an equal number of gold and silver medals, but more bronze to accommodate the sports that award bronze to both semi-finalists who do not make the finals. Each medallist also received the traditional Birks blue box, lined with grey velvet, to protect their prized possession.

	MEDALS BY COUNTRY					MEDALS BY SPORT			
COUNTRY		GOLD	SILVER	BRONZE	TOTAL	COUNTRY	GOLD	SILVER	BRONZE	TOTAL

	MEDALS BY COUNTRY				
	COUNTRY	GOLD	SILVER	BRONZE	TOTAL
1	United States	106	110	80	296
2	Canada	64	52	80	196
3	Cuba	69	40	47	156
4	Brazil	25	32	44	101
5	Argentina	25	19	28	72
6	Mexico	11	16	30	57
7	Colombia	7	17	18	42
8	Venezuela	7	16	17	40
9	Jamaica	3	4	6	13
10	Puerto Rico	1	3	9	13
11	Chile	1	3	7	11
12	Dominican Rep.	1	3	5	9
13	Ecuador	1	2	5	8
14	Peru	0	2	6	8
15	Guatemala	2	1	1	4
16	Uruguay	0	1	3	4
17	Bahamas	2	0	1	3
18	Bermuda	1	2	0	3
19	Suriname	1	0	1	2
20	Barbados	0	1	1	2
20	Panama	0	1	1	2
22	Netherland Antilles	1	0	0	1
23	Cayman Islands	0	1	0	1
23	Honduras	0	1	0	1
25	Costa Rica	0	0	1	1
25	El Salvador	0	0	1	1
25	Trinidad & Tobago	0	0	1	1

MEDALS BY SPORT

ARCHERY

COUNTRY	GOLD	SILVER	BRONZE	TOTAL
Canada	0	1	0	1
Chile	0	1	0	1
Cuba	1	1	1	3
Mexico	0	0	1	1
United States	3	1	2	6

ARTISTIC GYMNASTIC

COUNTRY	GOLD	SILVER	BRONZE	TOTAL
Argentina	1	2	1	4
Brazil	0	1	2	3
Canada	5	4	2	11
Colombia	0	1	1	2
Cuba	7	3	2	12
Puerto Rico	0	0	2	2
United States	1	2	2	5
Venezuela	0	1	2	3

ATHLETICS

COUNTRY	GOLD	SILVER	BRONZE	TOTAL
Argentina	2	0	1	3
Bahamas	2	0	1	3
Barbados	0	1	1	2
Brazil	7	5	4	16

COUNTRY	GOLD	SILVER	BRONZE	TOTAL
Canada	4	2	9	15
Cayman Islands	0	1	0	1
Chile	1	0	1	2
Colombia	0	3	1	4
Cuba	10	9	5	24
Ecuador	0	0	1	1
Jamaica	3	1	4	8
Mexico	7	4	1	12
Suriname	1	0	0	1
United States	10	18	16	44
Uruguay	0	0	1	1
Venezuela	0	1	0	1

BADMINTON

COUNTRY	GOLD	SILVER	BRONZE	TOTAL
Canada	3	4	3	10
Guatemala	0	0	1	1
Mexico	0	0	1	1
Peru	0	0	3	3
United States	2	1	2	5

BASEBALL

COUNTRY	GOLD	SILVER	BRONZE	TOTAL
Canada	0	0	1	1
Cuba	1	0	0	1
United States	0	1	0	1

BASKETBALL

COUNTRY	GOLD	SILVER	BRONZE	TOTAL
Brazil	1	0	0	1
Canada	0	1	0	1
Cuba	1	0	0	1
Puerto Rico	0	0	1	1
United States	0	1	1	2

BEACH VOLLEYBALL

COUNTRY	GOLD	SILVER	BRONZE	TOTAL
Brazil	1	1	1	3
Canada	1	0	0	1
Mexico	0	0	1	1
United States	0	1	0	1

BOXING

COUNTRY	GOLD	SILVER	BRONZE	TOTAL
Argentina	2	0	3	5
Brazil	0	2	2	4
Canada	0	5	1	6
Colombia	0	0	1	1
Cuba	9	0	3	12
Ecuador	0	0	1	1

COUNTRY	GOLD	SILVER	BRONZE	TOTAL
Jamaica	0	0	2	2
Mexico	0	1	3	4
Puerto Rico	0	0	1	1
United States	1	3	4	8
Venezuela	0	1	3	4

CANOE/KAYAK

COUNTRY	GOLD	SILVER	BRONZE	TOTAL
Argentina	3	1	0	4
Brazil	0	2	3	5
Canada	4	3	1	8
Cuba	3	3	3	9
Mexico	0	0	1	1
United States	2	3	4	9

CYCLING

COUNTRY	GOLD	SILVER	BRONZE	TOTAL
Argentina	1	1	3	5
Brazil	0	0	2	2
Canada	4	3	2	9
Chile	0	0	1	1
Colombia	1	2	2	5
Cuba	1	3	5	9
Mexico	0	3	0	3
Trinidad & Tobago	0	0	1	1
United States	11	6	1	18
Uruguay	0	0	1	1

| 213

VOLUNTEERS

DIVING

COUNTRY	GOLD	SILVER	BRONZE	TOTAL
Canada	2	1	1	4
Cuba	0	1	0	1
Mexico	1	1	2	4
United States	1	1	1	3

EQUESTRIAN

COUNTRY	GOLD	SILVER	BRONZE	TOTAL
Bermuda	1	0	0	1
Brazil	1	1	1	3
Canada	1	1	1	3
Colombia	0	1	0	1
Mexico	0	0	2	2
United States	3	3	1	7

FENCING

COUNTRY	GOLD	SILVER	BRONZE	TOTAL
Argentina	0	0	1	1
Canada	1	1	3	5
Chile	0	1	0	1
Colombia	0	0	1	1

COUNTRY	GOLD	SILVER	BRONZE	TOTAL
Cuba	9	3	2	14
Mexico	0	1	1	2
Puerto Rico	0	1	0	1
United States	0	2	5	7
Venezuela	0	1	2	3

FIELD HOCKEY

COUNTRY	GOLD	SILVER	BRONZE	TOTAL
Argentina	1	1	0	2
Canada	1	0	1	2
Cuba	0	0	1	1
United States	0	1	0	1

JUDO

COUNTRY	GOLD	SILVER	BRONZE	TOTAL
Argentina	1	2	4	7
Brazil	1	3	6	10
Canada	1	1	4	6
Cuba	9	1	4	14
Dominican Rep.	0	0	2	2
Ecuador	0	0	1	1
Mexico	0	0	1	1
Puerto Rico	0	2	0	2
United States	2	2	5	9
Venezuela	0	3	1	4

KARATE

COUNTRY	GOLD	SILVER	BRONZE	TOTAL
Brazil	1	4	3	8
Canada	0	0	2	2
Colombia	0	1	0	1
Cuba	2	0	3	5
Dominican Rep.	0	1	0	1
Ecuador	0	0	1	1
Mexico	0	1	4	5
Netherlands Antilles	1	0	0	1
Peru	0	1	2	3
United States	5	1	3	9
Uruguay	0	0	1	1
Venezuela	2	2	3	7

MODERN PENTATHLON

COUNTRY	GOLD	SILVER	BRONZE	TOTAL
Canada	0	0	1	1
Mexico	0	1	1	2
United States	2	1	0	3

VOLUNTEERS

RACQUETBALL

COUNTRY	GOLD	SILVER	BRONZE	TOTAL
Canada	0	3	0	3
Chile	0	0	1	1
Mexico	0	0	1	1
Puerto Rico	0	0	1	1
United States	4	1	1	6

RYTHMIC GYMNASTICS

COUNTRY	GOLD	SILVER	BRONZE	TOTAL
Brazil	1	0	0	1
Canada	1	0	1	2
Cuba	0	1	1	2
United States	0	1	0	1

ROLLER SPORTS

COUNTRY	GOLD	SILVER	BRONZE	TOTAL
Argentina	4	3	1	8
Brazil	0	0	4	4
Canada	0	0	1	1
Colombia	1	3	3	7
United States	6	4	2	12
Uruguay	0	1	0	1

ROWING

COUNTRY	GOLD	SILVER	BRONZE	TOTAL
Argentina	7	1	0	8
Brazil	0	1	0	1
Canada	4	2	4	10
Chile	0	0	2	2
Cuba	0	2	6	8
Mexico	0	1	0	1
United States	3	7	2	12

SAILING

COUNTRY	GOLD	SILVER	BRONZE	TOTAL
Argentina	2	0	2	4
Bermuda	0	2	0	2
Brazil	1	5	3	9
Canada	3	1	2	6
Cuba	1	0	0	1
Mexico	0	0	1	1
Puerto Rico	1	0	0	1
United States	2	2	2	6

SHOOTING

COUNTRY	GOLD	SILVER	BRONZE	TOTAL
Argentina	1	1	1	3
Brazil	0	0	1	1
Canada	1	2	5	8
Colombia	1	0	3	4
Cuba	1	0	2	3
Guatemala	1	0	0	1
Mexico	0	0	1	1
United States	9	9	1	19
Venezuela	0	2	0	2

SOCCER

COUNTRY	GOLD	SILVER	BRONZE	TOTAL
Costa Rica	0	0	1	1
Honduras	0	1	0	1
Mexico	1	1	0	2
United States	1	0	1	2

SOFTBALL

COUNTRY	GOLD	SILVER	BRONZE	TOTAL
Canada	1	1	0	2
Cuba	0	0	2	2
United States	1	1	0	2

SQUASH

COUNTRY	GOLD	SILVER	BRONZE	TOTAL
Argentina	0	1	2	3
Brazil	0	1	2	3
Canada	4	0	1	5
Colombia	0	0	1	1
Mexico	0	0	1	1
United States	0	2	1	3

SWIMMING

COUNTRY	GOLD	SILVER	BRONZE	TOTAL
Argentina	0	2	1	3
Brazil	7	3	5	15
Canada	13	5	14	32
Cuba	1	0	1	2
Jamaica	0	3	0	3
Panama	0	1	0	1
Suriname	0	0	1	1
United States	10	19	8	37
Venezuela	1	0	2	3

SYNCHRONIZED SWIMMING

COUNTRY	GOLD	SILVER	BRONZE	TOTAL
Brazil	0	0	1	1
Canada	2	0	0	2
Mexico	0	0	1	1
United States	0	2	0	2

TABLE TENNIS

COUNTRY	GOLD	SILVER	BRONZE	TOTAL
Argentina	0	2	0	2
Brazil	0	0	2	2
Canada	0	2	2	4
Chile	0	0	2	2
Cuba	0	0	1	1
United States	4	0	1	5

TAEKWONDO

COUNTRY	GOLD	SILVER	BRONZE	TOTAL
Argentina	0	0	2	2
Canada	1	1	4	6
Cuba	1	2	2	5
Dominican Rep.	0	1	1	2
Ecuador	0	0	1	1

COUNTRY	GOLD	SILVER	BRONZE	TOTAL
Guatemala	1	0	0	1
Mexico	2	1	1	4
Puerto Rico	0	0	2	2
United States	1	1	3	5
Venezuela	2	2	0	4

TEAM HANDBALL

COUNTRY	GOLD	SILVER	BRONZE	TOTAL
Argentina	0	0	1	1
Brazil	1	1	0	2
Canada	0	1	0	1
Cuba	1	0	1	2

TENNIS

COUNTRY	GOLD	SILVER	BRONZE	TOTAL
Argentina	0	0	3	3
Brazil	2	0	1	3
Canada	0	0	1	1
Chile	0	1	0	1
Mexico	0	1	0	1
United States	1	2	2	5
Venezuela	1	0	1	2

TENPIN BOWLING

COUNTRY	GOLD	SILVER	BRONZE	TOTAL
Canada	0	1	2	3
Colombia	1	1	0	2
Mexico	0	0	2	2
United States	3	1	0	4
Venezuela	0	1	0	1

TRIATHLON

COUNTRY	GOLD	SILVER	BRONZE	TOTAL
Brazil	0	1	0	1
Canada	1	0	2	3
United States	0	1	0	1
Venezuela	1	0	0	1

VOLLEYBALL

COUNTRY	GOLD	SILVER	BRONZE	TOTAL
Brazil	1	1	0	2
Canada	0	0	1	1
Cuba	1	1	0	2
United States	0	0	1	1

WATER POLO

COUNTRY	GOLD	SILVER	BRONZE	TOTAL
Brazil	0	0	1	1
Canada	1	0	1	2
Cuba	0	1	0	1
United States	1	1	0	2

WATER SKIING

COUNTRY	GOLD	SILVER	BRONZE	TOTAL
Argentina	0	1	2	3
Canada	2	3	1	6
Colombia	0	0	1	1
Mexico	0	0	1	1
United States	4	2	1	7

WEIGHTLIFTING

COUNTRY	GOLD	SILVER	BRONZE	TOTAL
Argentina	0	1	0	1
Canada	2	1	1	4
Colombia	2	6	3	11
Cuba	4	2	0	6
Dominican Rep.	1	1	2	4

COUNTRY	GOLD	SILVER	BRONZE	TOTAL
El Salvador	0	0	1	1
Guatemala	0	0	1	1
Mexico	0	0	1	1
Panama	0	0	1	1
Puerto Rico	0	0	1	1
United States	5	1	3	9
Venezuela	0	1	1	2

WRESTLING

COUNTRY	GOLD	SILVER	BRONZE	TOTAL
Canada	1	2	5	8
Colombia	0	0	1	1
Cuba	7	7	2	16
Mexico	0	0	1	1
Peru	0	1	1	2
Puerto Rico	0	0	1	1
United States	8	5	3	16
Venezuela	0	1	2	3

FRIENDS OF THE '99 GAMES

The Friends of the Games fundraising initiative was developed to provide Manitoba Businesses with the opportunity to become involved with the Pan American Games. The program was a vehiclefor businesses to demonstrate their participation in, commitment to, and and support of their community.

3M Canada Corporation
Acklands Grainger
Adolph Kiefer & Associates
Advance Electronics
Advantage Sport Athletic Services
Aikins, MacAulay & Thorvaldson
Allco Electrical Ltd.
Apotex Inc.
AON Reed Stenhouse
Aramark
B.A. Robinson Ltd.
Baxter Corporation
Becton Dickinson Canada
Bermo Imports
Birchwood Automotive Group
Bituminex Limited
BLOCKBUSTER Video Canada Inc.
Boeing CanadaBristol Aerospace Ltd.
Browning Ferris Industries
Brunswick Steel
Cambrian Excavators
Campbell North Rentals
Canada Moving
CanWest Global Communications
Cargill Limited
CBC Radio
Ceridian Canada Ltd.
Certified General Accountants Association
Charter House Hotel
Concept Fiatlux Inc.
Concord Projects
Contact Management Group
Conviron
Correct Craft Inc.
CORPAV Presentation Group
Cummins Mid Canada Ltd.
/Mid Canada Thermo King
Daktronics
Deloitte & Touche LLP
Dimension Display
Dominion Construction Company
Dominion Tanners
Domo Gasoline Corporation Ltd.
Double 'B' Paving
Duboff Edwards Haight & Schachter
Dubois Motor Sport
Dufresne Furniture & Appliances

DUHA Color Services
Dunn-Rite Foods
E.H. Price Limited
Ernst & Young
Ernst Hansch Construction
Esdale Printing
Fillmore Riley
Fitness Experience/Bodyguard Fitness
Florist Supply
Forest Park Electric
Forks North Portage Partnership
Fort Gary Industries Ltd.
FWS Construction Ltd.
Gemini Fashions of Canada Ltd.
Geo H. Young & Co.
Gerdeau MRM Steel
Global Electric Motor Cars
Globe General Agencies
Green Gates Country Club
Grower Direct Florists - McPhillips Street
Guertin Equipment Ltd.
Hertz Certified Rentals
Hill Abra & Dewar
Hotel Fort Gary
ICG Propane
Inner Tec Security Services
Isobord Enterprises Inc.
Jet Auto Centre
JJH McLean Pianos
KORTEX Computer Centre
KPMG LLP Accountant
La Liberte
Landstar Development
Laufman Blueprinting Services
Le Beaujolais
LGM Graphics/Spot Graphics
Loran International Technologies Inc.
MacDon Industries
Man Shield Construction
Manitoba Chicken Producer Board
Manitoba Egg Producers
Manitoba Moose
Maple Leaf Construction Ltd.
Maple Leaf Foodservice
Master Lock Company
McCain Foods Canada
McCaine Electric Ltd.

McDiarmid Lumber Ltd.
McEwen Bros.
McKim Communications Ltd.
MediaTouch
Melet Plastics Inc.
Microsoft Canada Co.
Mister B's Marineland
Mitchell Fabrics
Moffat Communications Ltd.
Monsanto Canada Inc.
Moore North America
Mordens of Winnipeg Candy Mfg. Ltd.
Motor Coach Industries
National Leasing Group Inc.
ND Graphics Limited
Nelson River Construction Inc.
NewFlyer Industries
Nisby Home Renovations
North West Company
Norwood Hotel
Novopharm
Old Dutch Foods Ltd.
Online Business Systems
Paddle Wheel River Rouge Tours
Palmer Jarvis Communications
Pasta La Vista
PCL Constructors Canada Inc.
Peak of the Market
Perfect Pass Control Systems Inc.
Petro Canada
Pharmasave Drugs
Pimicikamak Cree Nation
Piston Ring Service
Pitblado Buchwald Asper
Pollard Banknote Limited
Portage Cartage & Storage
Pourex Ltd.
Powell Equipment Ltd.
POWERWARE Canada Inc.
Prendiville Industries
PriceWaterhouseCoopers
Qualico Developments
R.S. Harris Transport Ltd.
Rae and Jerry's Steak House
Red Lobster Canada
Residential Management Software
Rostin Sport

Royal LePage
Scaffold Connection Corporation
Schedule Masters Inc.
Select Sport
Shapes Fitness Centres
Shelter Canadian Properties Ltd.
Sheraton Winnipeg Hotel
Shindico
Sinclair Dental Company Ltd.
Smith & Nephew Inc.
South Side Autobody
Spieth Anderson International
Standard Aero
TARAFLEX
Taylor McCaffrey
Tentnology
Terrecon Developments
The Bowering Group
The Inland Group
The Keg Steakhouse & Bar
The Lombard
The Old Spaghetti Factory
Thompson Dorfman Sweatman
TransCanada Pipelines
True Value Hardware
and V & S Department Stores
UCS SpiritVision Security & Investigations Inc.
Wakshinsky Bros. Ltd.
Wallace & Wallace Fences
Wardrop Engineering
Werners Wholesale Group
Western Display Service Ltd.
Western Glove Works Ltd.
Western Opinion Research
Westsun International
Wilder Wilder & Langtry
Windsor Plywood
Winnipeg Building & Decorating
Winnipeg Commodity Exchange
Winnipeg Real Estate Board
Winpak
XCAN Grain Pool Ltd.
YONEX
York Barbell Company

VOLUNTEERS

CARGILL LIMITED

The 1999 Pan Am Games awakened us all to the spirit of Winnipeg, renewing our sense of community and revitalizing the future of Manitoba sport. Cargill was proud to sponsor this event as part of the Friends of the '99 Games program.

Cargill strives to support events that will enhance living standards in the communities where we live and work. The Pan Am Games brought the excitement of world class competition to Winnipeg and left behind a legacy of sporting facilities and scholarships for the young people of Manitoba and Canada.

Kerry Hawkins, President of Cargill Limited, was pleased to serve as chairman of the Friends of the Games fund-raising committee. The committee was able to exceed its goals, through the generous support of Manitoba's business community.

Nutrena Feeds, part of Cargill's Animal Nutrition Division, was named as the principal feed supplier for the Pan Am equestrian events, preparing and delivering high quality feed to horses from across the Americas.

Cargill would like to congratulate all the organizers, volunteers and fellow Friends of the Games on their hard work and vision in planning and putting on this event. We are proud and privileged to have shared in the Pan Am experience.

WINNIPEG COMMODITY EXCHANGE

Winnipeg Commodity Exchange was proud to sponsor this millennium's final Pan American Games. The Exchange is always pleased to welcome international visitors to our province. We hosted numerous tours of our trading floor for interested Pan Am participants, and WCE employees volunteered their time and talents in support of the Games. Congratulations to all the athletes, volunteers, organizers and others for creating such good memories of sportsmanship and spirit!

Established in 1887, Winnipeg Commodity Exchange (WCE) is Canada's only agricultural futures and options exchange. Situated in the heart of the Canadian Prairies, the historic centre of North America's grain trade, WCE provides price discovery and risk management tools for domestic and international market participants. It is a not-for-profit membership organization, including international grain firms, grain handling companies, domestic merchants, exporters, processors, brokerage firms, financial institutions, producers and independent traders.

VOLUNTEERS

GEMINI FASHIONS OF CANADA LTD.

Gemini Fashions of Canada Ltd. is actively involved in supplying outerwear for the sports enthusiast and is proud to have supported the very successful Pan American Games. Founded in 1971, Gemini, headquartered in Winnipeg, has grown to become Canada's leading diversified outerwear supplier. With manufacturing capabilities both in Winnipeg and abroad, Gemini satisfies outerwear requirements for both the Canadian and international markets.

While our capabilities include private label development for industrial and strategic international and Canadian customers, we feature a number of high profile brands from children's outerwear to authentic skiwear for the multi-discipline athlete in the Sun Ice line. The northern Sun outerwear line features First Nation's themes; Gemini Sport provides casual women's wear for today's lifestyle. Technical outerwear for snow sports needs and SkiGem, durable and fashionable apparel for the active youth, round out Gemini's top brands.

EDITORIAL ACKNOWLEDGMENTS

Many thanks to the Winnipeg Fress Press and the following writers for their editorial contributions to this publication in the spirit of the Games.

SETTING THE STAGE

A History of Winnipeg's Bid	Jeffrey Tiessen, A Tribute to Champions
The Corporate Foundation	Jeffrey Tiessen, A Tribute to Champions
The Look of the Games	Tiffany Morris, A Tribute to Champions
The Spirit of '67	J.M. Bumsted, St. John's College, Winnipeg
	Paul Edmonds, Winnipeg Real Estate News

SPIRIT OF SPORT

A Historical Journey	Tiffany Morris, A Tribute to Champions
A Passion for Pins	Kimberly Tiessen, A Tribute to Champions
Air Watch	Linda Quattrin, Assistant City Editor, Winnipeg Free Press
Dignity & Grace	Lindor Reynolds, Winnipeg Free Press
Let the Games Begin	Kimberly Tiessen, A Tribute to Champions
Like Kids in a Candy Store	Maureen Littlejohn, Winnipeg Free Press
Mosquito Land	Kimberly Tiessen, A Tribute to Champions
Pan A'maniacs	Lindor Reynolds, Winnipeg Free Press
Summer Cleaning	David O'Brien, City Hall Reporter, Winnipeg Free Press
The Littlest Helper	Kimberly Tiessen, A Tribute to Champions
The Salmon People	Leah Janzen and Kim Guttormson, Winnipeg Free Press
Unscheduled Pit Stops	Kim Guttormson, Winnipeg Fress Press
Village Stars	Duncan Morrison, Pan Am Contributor
Who's Got Tickets?	Tiffany Morris, A Tribute to Champions
Winnipeg Proud	Randy Turner, Winnipeg Free Press
Winnipeg's Golden Girl	Kimberly Tiessen, A Tribute to Champions
Young at Heart	Kimberly Tiessen, A Tribute to Champions

THE COMPETITION

Beach Balls	Tiffany Morris, A Tribute to Champions
Black Monday	Buzz Currie, Winnipeg Free Press
Brazilians Crowned Kings	Dan Lett, Winnipeg Free Press
Changing of the Guard	Tiffany Morris, A Tribute to Champions
Choreography, Grace & Gold	Allison Bray, Winnipeg Free Press
Emerging Star	Jason Bell, Pan Am Contributor
Fight Night at Duckworth	Tiffany Morris, A Tribute to Champions
Fighting Her Own Battle	David Kuxhaus, Winnipeg Free Press
Fool's Gold	Kimberly Tiessen, A Tribute to Champions

Heart of Gold	David O'Brien, Winnipeg Free Press
Hell on Wheels	Kimberly Tiessen, A Tribute to Champions
Here's to You Emma Robinson	Helen Fallding, Winnipeg Free Press
Hitting the Mark	Paul McKie, Winnipeg Free Press
Lady luck...	Alexandra Paul, Winnipeg Free Press
Life in the Fast Lane	Randy Turner, Winnipeg Free Press
One Last Splash	Aldo Smith, Winnipeg Free Press
Pressure Front and Center	Tiffany Morris, A Tribute to Champions
Proud Canadians	Kimberly Tiessen, A Tribute to Champions
Sight of a Lifetime	Kimberly Tiessen, A Tribute to Champions
Sport of Kings	Alexandra Paul, Winnipeg Free Press
Sword Point	Bill Redekop, Winnipeg Free Press
Table Talk	Morley Walker, Winnipeg Free Press
The Bowling Sebelen Family	Duncan Morrison, Winnipeg Free Press
Thrill of Victory	Kimberly Tiessen, A Tribute to Champions
Tiny Island Makes History	Chris Cariou, Sports Reporter
Triathlete Takes Flight	Tiffany Morris, A Tribute to Champions
Victory for Venezuela's Vento	Ross Romaniuk, Winnipeg Free Press
Weathering the Storm	Ross Romaniuk, Pan Am Reporter
You're Speaking my Language	Bud Robertson, Winnipeg Free Press

LEGACY

21st Century Pan Ams	Leah Janzen, Winnipeg Free Press
A Farewell to the Americas	Tiffany Morris, A Tribute to Champions
And That's the News	Kimberly Tiessen, A Tribute to Champions
Hot Stuff	Jeffrey Tiessen, A Tribute to Champions
In the Wake of the Games	Jeffrey Tiessen, A Tribute to Champions
Pan Am Stamps	Tiffany Morris, A Tribute to Champions
Pan American Women	Leah Janzen and Kim Guttormson, Winnipeg Free Press
Preventative Medicine	Jeffrey Tiessen, A Tribute to Champions
Sharing the Dream	Tiffany Morris, A Tribute to Champions
With Glowing Hearts	Lindor Reynolds, Winnipeg Free Press

CULTURAL FESTIVAL

New Creation Project	Tiffany Morris, A Tribute to Champions
Where the Americas Came	Tiffany Morris, A Tribute to Champions

lver • James Koenig • Sylvia Lomow • Terri Jablonski • Sandra Isaac • Edward Barnes • Danielle Cadieux • William Goodwin • Judy Baker • Judy Baker • Charna Gilman • Kirsten Gibson • Ralph Backç • Maria Garcea • Kenneth Ponton • KellyLynn Beech • Sid Garvie • Trudy Alexander • Carla Friesen • Ted Foreman • Shelley Basaraba • Harvey Dyck • Cathy D'Andrea • Patricia Alexander • Derek Sutherland • Gladwyn Scott • Joelle Savard • Doren Roberts • Margaret Proven • Robert Potter • Kerry Pollock • Patrick
re • Patrick Moore • Roger MacDearmid • Gilbert Johnson • Bernie Mumaghan • Ella Licorish • Linda Wong • Linda Wong • Brent Jervis • Frank Friesen • Frank Friesen • Ruth Ziegler • Sandra Hobday • Susan Slater • Randy Hull • Donna Friesen • Dawn Fedowich • Barbara Wilson • David Ross • Paul Tomlinson • Dennis Reid • David Blatz • Ryan Gulakow • Maxine Pich • Jane Van Dam • Helen Peters • Helen Peters • William Girling • Carolyn Peck • Lauren Penny • Barbara Belanger • Brenda
s • Angelica Noakes • Larry Chornoboy • Rachael Mosley • Beth Mungal • Jennifer Adams • Gail Michalkow • Harry Beaton • Harry Beaton • Harry Beaton • Jack Meller • Gisele Meilleur • Heather McDougall • Jackie McGowan • Walter Murray • Denise Moller • Elaine Thompson • Alan McTavish • Erin Tertoch Harris • Andrea Martens • Colleen Johnson • JoAnne Marcoux • Gloria Grubega • Barbara Smith • Brian Fox • Hedie Epp • Marcel Lecuyer • Thomas Schultz • Lorna Law • Lorna Law • John Sawatzky
la Devine • Dan Rosin • John Deschamps • Loren Remillard • Valerie ChalainWhite • Deborah KauenhofenPenner • TerriLynn Pfitzner • Rosemarie Campbell • Sergio Pardini • Rob Johnstone • Douglas Johnston • Kenneth Packer • Alice Rueda • Alice Rueda • Patricia Cooper • Walter Kremers • Jean Coles • Wilson Ho • Dorothy Carswell • Gabe Langlois • David Carr • Katherine Kirk • Bert Friesen • Enid Butler • Charles Jones • Karen Flanigan • Karen Flanigan • Heather Brydon • Jim Fedorowich • Jim Fedorowich
ouamek Quangtakoune • Irving Cosgrove • Jean Boorman • Frank Conway • Mildred Bjarnason • Laurence Fields • Maurice Dendenault • Shamit Bal • Leonard Andrews • James Anderson • Arlene Karaz • Daphne Williams • Bruce Sloane • Cathy Garvie • Gerald Koroscil • Gerald Koroscil • June Wilson • Debbie Faurschou • Muriel Gambrel • Marion Murphy • Janice Williamson • Larry MacKenzie • Jacquelene Goodman • Jacquelene Goodman • Virginia Tumilson • Arlan Leano • Mary Gigliotti •

07/23/99 ~ 08/08/99

Games Sponsors

 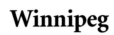

 **Panasonic**

 XEROX

 IBM. Great-West Life Kodak

Mondo America Inc. ~ Grand & Toy ~ EDS Systemhouse Inc. ~ Coca-Cola Bottling Ltd. ~ GeoLogistics Co. ~ Air Canada
The Perrier Group ~ Labatt Breweries of Canada ~ James Richardson International ~ Canada Post Corporation
Musco Sport Lighting Inc. ~ Palliser Furniture Ltd. ~ Sportec ~ Henry Birks & Sons Ltd. ~ Tim Hortons

Manitoba Public Insurance ~ Wawanesa Insurance ~ CJOB 68 ~ Winnipeg Airports Authority
Manitoba Lotteries Corporation ~ Winnipeg Free Press ~ The Bay / Zellers

Dan Galbraith